M000251516

Aircraft Weight and Balance Handbook

2016

U.S. Department of Transportation
FEDERAL AVIATION ADMINISTRATION
Flight Standards Service

Preface

The Aircraft Weight and Balance Handbook has been prepared in recognition of the importance of weight and balance technology in conducting safe and efficient flight. The objective of this handbook is twofold: to provide the airframe and powerplant mechanic (A&P) with the method of determining the empty weight and empty weight center of gravity (EWCG) of an aircraft and to furnish the flight crew with information on loading and operating the aircraft to ensure its weight is within the allowable limit and the center of gravity (CG) is within the allowable range.

Any time there is a conflict between the information in this handbook and specific information issued by an aircraft manufacturer, the manufacturer's data takes precedence over information in this handbook. Occasionally, the word "must" or similar language is used where the desired action is deemed critical. The use of such language is not intended to add to, interpret, or relieve a duty imposed by Title 14 of the Code of Federal Regulations (14 CFR).

It is essential for persons using this handbook to become familiar with and apply the pertinent parts of 14 CFR. The current Flight Standards Service airman training and testing material and learning statements for all airman certificates and ratings can be obtained from www.faa.gov.

This handbook supersedes FAA-H-8083-1A, Aircraft Weight and Balance Handbook, dated 2007.

This handbook is available for download, in PDF format, from www.faa.gov.

This handbook is published by the United States Department of Transportation, Federal Aviation Administration, Airman Testing Standards Branch, AFS-630, P.O. Box 25082, Oklahoma City, OK 73125.

Comments regarding this publication should be sent, in email form, to the following address:

AFS630comments@faa.gov.

John S. Duncan
Director, Flight Standards Service

Introduction

This handbook begins with the basic principle of aircraft weight and balance control, emphasizing its importance and including examples of documentation furnished by the aircraft manufacturer and by the FAA to ensure the aircraft weight and balance records contain the proper data.

Procedures for the preparation and the actual weighing of an aircraft are described, as are the methods of determining the location of the empty weight center of gravity (EWCG) relative to both the datum and the mean aerodynamic chord (MAC).

Loading computations for general aviation aircraft are discussed using both loading graphs and tables of weight and moment indexes.

Information is included that allows an FAA-certificated mechanic or repairman to determine the weight and center of gravity (CG) changes caused by repairs and alterations or removal and installation of equipment. This includes instructions for conducting adverse-loaded CG checks, also explaining the way to determine the amount and location of ballast needed to bring the CG within allowable limits.

The unique requirements for helicopter weight and balance control are discussed, including the determination of lateral CG and the way both lateral and longitudinal CG change as fuel is consumed.

One chapter includes the methods and examples of solving weight and balance problems using a hand-held electronic calculator, E6-B flight computer, and a dedicated electronic flight computer.

Acknowledgments

The Aircraft Weight and Balance Handbook (FAA-H-8083-1B) was produced by the Federal Aviation Administration (FAA) with the assistance of Safety Research Corporation of America (SRCA). The FAA wishes to acknowledge the following contributors:

Larry Jackson of Jackson Aircraft Weighing Service, for content and photographs used in Chapter 3

The White Planes Picture Company (www.whiteplanes.com), for images used in Chapter 4

Terri Sipantzi of Precision Windsports, for the weight-shift control sample weight and loading diagram used in Chapter 4

AirBorne Windsports Pty Ltd., for weight-shift control sample weight and loading data sheet used in Chapter 4

Jim Stevens of Aerosports Connection, for powered parachute sample weight and balance information sheet used in Chapter 4

Sporty's Pilot Shop, for image of an E6B Flight Computer used in Chapter 10

Table of Contents

Preface...iii

Introduction..v

Acknowledgments...vii

Table of Contents ix

Chapter 1
Weight and Balance Control............................1-1
Introduction...1-1
Responsibility for Weight and Balance Control 1-2
Terminology..1-2
Weight Control 1-2
Effects of Weight 1-3
Weight Changes 1-3
Stability and Balance Control 1-4
Weight Control for Aircraft Other Than Fixed and
Rotor-wing 1-5
   Weight-Shift Control Aircraft 1-5
   Powered Parachutes..1-6
   Balloons...1-6
Underestimating the Importance of Weight and
Balance..1-6

Chapter 2
Weight and Balance Theory 2-1
Introduction...2-1
Weight and Balance Theory......................................2-2
   Arm 2-2
   Moment 2-2
The Law of the Lever...2-2
Shifting the Balance Point or CG................................2-4
   Solution by Chart 2-4
   Basic Weight and Balance Equation 2-4
   Solution by Formula...2-5
Mean Aerodynamic Chord...2-5
FAA-Furnished Weight and Balance Information 2-6
   CG Range 2-6
   Empty Weight CG Range (EWCG) 2-6

   Maximum Weights 2-6
   Number of Seats 2-6
   Maximum Baggage 2-6
   Fuel Capacity..2-6
   Oil Capacity (Wet Sump)...................................2-6
   Data Pertinent to all Models...............................2-10
Manufacturer-Furnished Information 2-10

Chapter 3
**Weighing the Aircraft and Determining the
Empty Weight Center of Gravity 3-1**
Introduction...3-1
Requirements 3-2
Equipment for Weighing...3-2
Preparation for Weighing..3-3
   Scale Preparation 3-3
   Weigh Clean Aircraft Inside Hangar.....................3-4
   Equipment List 3-4
   Ballast...3-4
   Standard Weights 3-4
   Draining the Fuel...3-4
   Oil..3-4
   Other Fluids..3-4
   Configuration of the Aircraft...............................3-5
   Jacking the Aircraft 3-5
   Leveling the Aircraft 3-5
   Safety Considerations.......................................3-5
Determining the CG..3-5
EWCG Formulas..3-6
   Datum Forward of the Airplane—Nosewheel
   Landing Gear..3-6
   Datum Aft of the Main Wheels—Nosewheel
   Landing Gear..3-6
Location of Datum 3-7
   Datum Forward of the Main Wheels—Tailwheel
   Landing Gear..3-7
   Datum Aft of the Main Wheels—Tailwheel
   Landing Gear..3-7
Center of Gravity (CG) and Mean Aerodynamic
Chord (MAC)..3-8

Center of Gravity (CG)..............................3-8

Mean Aerodynamic Chord (MAC) 3-8

Chapter 4
Light Sport Aircraft Weight and Balance Control..4-1
Introduction..4-1

LSA Definition of Terms...............................4-2

Weight and Balance 4-3

WSC Aircraft 4-3

Powered Parachutes...................................4-4

Weight and Balance Computations (Amateur-Built Aircraft)...4-4

Chapter 5
Single-Engine Aircraft Weight and Balance Computations 5-1
Introduction..5-1

Determining the Loaded Weight and CG 5-2

Manual Computational Method............................5-2

Loading Graph Method 5-4

Moment Indexes 5-4

Loading Graph 5-4

Compute Weight and Balance Using the Loading Graph 5-4

Chapter 6
Multiengine Aircraft Weight and Balance Computations 6-1
Introduction..6-1

Determine the Loaded CG 6-2

Chart Method Using Weight, Arm, and Moments 6-2

Determining the CG in Percentage of Mean Aerodynamic Chord (MAC) 6-3

The Chart Method Using Weight and Moment Indexes 6-3

Chapter 7
Center of Gravity Change After a Repair or Alteration 7-1
Introduction..7-1

Equipment List..7-2

Major Alteration and Repair 7-3

Weight and Balance Revision Record 7-3

Weight Changes Caused by a Repair or Alteration 7-5

Computations Using Weight, Arm, and Moment.......7-5

Computations Using Weight and Moment Indexes ...7-5

Determining the CG in Percentage of Mean Aerodynamic Chord (Percent MAC) 7-6

Empty Weight CG (EWCG) Range 7-6

Adverse-Load CG Checks 7-6

Forward Adverse-Load CG Check.........................7-7

Aft Adverse-Load CG Check 7-7

Ballast 7-7

Temporary Ballast 7-8

Temporary Ballast Formula..............................7-8

Permanent Ballast 7-8

Chapter 8
Weight and Balance Control—Helicopter 8-1
Introduction..8-1

Determining the Loaded CG of a Helicopter 8-3

Effects of Offloading Passengers and Using Fuel..........8-3

Chapter 9
Weight and Balance Control—Commuter Category and Large Aircraft 9-1
Introduction..9-1

Establishing the Initial Weight of an Aircraft 9-2

Determining the Empty Weight and Empty Weight CG (EWCG)..9-2

Documenting Changes to an Aircraft's Weight and Balance 9-3

Determining the Loaded CG of the Airplane in Percent MAC 9-3

Operational Empty Weight (OEW) 9-5

Reestablishing the OEW 9-5

Fleet Operating Empty Weights (FOEW) 9-5

Onboard Aircraft Weighing System.......................9-5

Determining the Correct Stabilizer Trim Setting 9-6

Determining CG Changes Caused by Modifying the Cargo..9-6

Effects of Loading or Offloading Cargo 9-6

Effects of Shifting Cargo From One Hold to Another...9-8

Determining Cargo Pallet Loads and Floor Loading Limits 9-9

Determining the Maximum Amount of Payload That Can Be Carried 9-10

Determining the Landing Weight..........................9-10

Determining Fuel Dump Time in Minutes 9-12

Weight and Balance of Commuter Category Airplanes 9-12

Determining the Loaded Weight and CG................9-12

Determining the Changes in CG When Passengers Are Shifted 9-16

Determining Changes in Weight and CG When the Aircraft Is Operated in Its Cargo Configuration..9-18

Determining the CG Shift When Cargo Is Moved From One Section to Another 9-18

Determining the CG Shift When Cargo Is Added or Removed 9-18

Determining Which Limits Are Exceeded 9-18

Chapter 10
Use of Computer for Weight and Balance
Computations **10-1**
Introduction...10-1
Electronic Calculator 10-2
E6-B Flight Computer..10-2
Dedicated Electronic Flight Computer 10-3
  Typical Weight and Balance Problems 10-4
  Determining CG in Inches From the Datum 10-4
    Nosewheel Airplane With Datum Ahead of the
    Main Wheels..10-4
    Nosewheel Airplane With Datum Behind the
    Main Wheels..10-4
    Tailwheel Airplane With Datum Ahead of the
    Main Wheels..10-4
    Tailwheel Airplane With Datum Behind the
    Main Wheels..10-4
  Determining CG, Given Weights, and Arms 10-5
  Determining CG, Given Weights, and Moment
  Indexes...10-5
  Determining CG in Percent Mean Aerodynamic
  Chord (MAC) 10-5
  Determining Lateral CG of a Helicopter.................10-5
  Determining ΔCG Caused by Shifting Weights.......10-6
  Determining Weight Shifted to Cause Specified
  ΔCG..10-6
  Determining Distance Weight Is Shifted to Move
  CG a Specific Distance...10-6
  Determining Total Weight of an Aircraft With a
  Specified ΔCG When Cargo Is Moved 10-7
  Determining Amount of Ballast Needed to Move
  CG to a Desired Location......................................10-7

Appendix A...**A-1**

Appendix B...**B-1**

Glossary **G-1**

Index **I-1**

Chapter 1
Weight and Balance Control

CG

Lift

Fixed
Nose-down force
independent of airspeed

Variable
Nose-up force
dependent upon airspeed

Introduction

There are many factors in the safe and efficient operation of aircraft, including proper weight and balance control. The weight and balance system commonly employed among aircraft consists of three equally important elements: the weighing of the aircraft, the maintaining of the weight and balance records, and the proper loading of the aircraft. An inaccuracy in any one of these elements defeats the purpose of the system. The final loading calculations are meaningless if either the aircraft has been improperly weighed or the records contain an error.

Improper loading decreases the efficiency and performance of an aircraft from the standpoint of altitude, maneuverability, rate of climb, and speed. It may even be the cause of failure to complete the flight or, for that matter, failure to start the flight. Because of abnormal stresses placed upon the structure of an improperly loaded aircraft, or because of changed flying characteristics of the aircraft, loss of life and destruction of valuable equipment may result.

Lift

CG

Insufficient elevator
Nose-down force

CG too far aft

Outboard fuel: tail heavy

Inboard fuel: nose heavy

Additional lift and drag

Empty

Full

Additional weight

CG

Lift

Insufficient elevator
Nose-up force

CG too far forward

Aircraft can perform safely and achieve their designed efficiency only when they are operated and maintained in the way their designers intended. This safety and efficiency is determined to a large degree by holding the aircraft's weight and balance parameters within the limits specified for its design. The remainder of this handbook describes how this is done.

Responsibility for Weight and Balance Control

The responsibility for proper weight and balance control begins with the engineers and designers and extends to the technicians who maintain the aircraft and the pilots who operate them. Modern aircraft are engineered utilizing state-of-the-art technology and materials to achieve maximum reliability and performance for the intended category. As much care and expertise must be exercised in operating and maintaining these efficient aircraft as was taken in their design and manufacturing:

1. The designers of an aircraft set the maximum weight based on the amount of lift the wings or rotors can provide under the operational conditions for which the aircraft is designed. The structural strength of the aircraft also limits the maximum weight the aircraft can safely carry. The designers carefully determine the ideal center of gravity (CG) and calculate the maximum allowable deviation from this specific location.

2. The manufacturer provides the aircraft operator with the empty weight of the aircraft and the location of its empty weight center of gravity (EWCG) at the time the certified aircraft leaves the factory. Amateur-built aircraft must have this information determined and available at the time of certification.

3. The FAA-certificated mechanic or repairman who maintains the aircraft keeps the weight and balance records current, recording any changes that have been made because of repairs or alterations.

4. The pilot in command (PIC) has the responsibility prior to every flight to know the maximum allowable weight of the aircraft and its CG limits. This allows the pilot to determine during the preflight inspection that the aircraft is loaded so that the CG is within the allowable limits.

Terminology

Pilots and FAA-certificated mechanics or repairmen must ensure they understand the terms as they relate to the aircraft in question. For small aircraft terminology, use the information found in sources associated with Civil Air Regulation (CAR) 3 certification or General Aviation Manufacturers Association (GAMA) Specification No. 1 for part 23 aircraft or part 27 for rotorcraft. For terminology applied to large part 25 aircraft, information can be found in Advisory Circular (AC) 120-27, Aircraft Weight and Balance Control. The glossary contains the most current terms and definitions. Current regulations are available from the Superintendent of Documents; U.S. Government Printing Office; Washington, DC 20402. They are also located on the FAA website at www.faa.gov. Earlier regulations may be available in libraries or in the Federal Register.

Weight Control

Weight is a major factor in airplane construction and operation, and it demands respect from all pilots and particular diligence by all maintenance personnel. Excessive weight reduces the efficiency of an aircraft and the available safety margin if an emergency condition should arise.

When an aircraft is designed, it is made as light as the required structural strength allows, and the wings or rotors are designed to support the maximum allowable weight. When the weight of an aircraft is increased, the wings or rotors must produce additional lift and the structure must support not only the additional static loads, but also the dynamic loads imposed by flight maneuvers. For example, the wings of a 3,000-pound airplane must support 3,000 pounds in level flight, but when the airplane is turned smoothly and sharply using a bank angle of 60°, the dynamic load requires the wings to support twice this or 6,000 pounds.

Severe uncoordinated maneuvers or flight into turbulence can impose dynamic loads on the structure great enough to cause failure. In accordance with Title 14 of the Code of Federal Regulations (14 CFR) part 23, the structure of a normal category airplane must be strong enough to sustain a load factor of 3.8 times its weight. Every pound of weight added to a normal category aircraft requires that the structure be strong enough to support 3.8 pounds. An aircraft operated in the utility category must sustain a load factor of 4.4 times its weight, and acrobatic category aircraft must be strong enough to withstand 6.0 times their weight.

The lift produced by a wing is determined by its airfoil shape, angle of attack, speed through the air, and air density. When an aircraft takes off from an airport with a high density altitude, it must accelerate to a speed faster than would be required at sea level to produce enough lift to allow takeoff; therefore, a longer takeoff run is necessary. The distance needed may be longer than the available runway. When operating from a high density altitude airport, the Pilot's Operating Handbook (POH) or Airplane Flight Manual (AFM) must be consulted to determine the maximum weight allowed for the aircraft under the conditions of altitude, temperature, wind, and runway conditions.

Effects of Weight

Most modern aircraft are so designed that, when all seats are occupied, the baggage compartment is full, and all fuel tanks are full, the aircraft is grossly overloaded. This type of design requires the pilot to give great consideration to the requirements of each specific flight. If maximum range is required, occupants or baggage must be left behind, or if the maximum load must be carried, the range, dictated by the amount of fuel on board, must be reduced.

Overloading an aircraft can create a variety of problems:

- The aircraft needs a higher takeoff speed, which results in a longer takeoff run.

- Both the rate and angle of climb are reduced.

- The service ceiling is lowered.

- The cruising speed is reduced.

- The cruising range is shortened.

- Maneuverability is decreased.

- A longer landing roll is required because the landing speed is higher.

- Excessive loads are imposed on the structure, especially the landing gear.

The POH or AFM includes tables or charts that give the pilot an indication of the performance expected for any weight. An important part of careful preflight planning includes a check of these charts to determine if the aircraft is loaded so the proposed flight can be safely made.

Weight Changes

The maximum allowable weight for an aircraft is determined by design considerations. However, the maximum operational weight may be less than the maximum allowable weight due to such considerations as high density altitude or high-drag field conditions caused by wet grass or water on the runway. The maximum operational weight may also be limited by the departure or arrival airport's runway length.

One important preflight consideration is the distribution of the load in the aircraft. Loading the aircraft so the gross weight is less than the maximum allowable is not enough. This weight must be distributed to keep the CG within the limits specified in the POH or AFM.

If the CG is too far forward, a heavy passenger can be moved to one of the rear seats or baggage may be shifted from a forward baggage compartment to a rear compartment. If the CG is too far aft, passenger weight or baggage can be shifted forward. The fuel load should be balanced laterally. The pilot

should pay special attention to the POH or AFM regarding the operation of the fuel system in order to keep the aircraft balanced in flight.

Weight and balance of a helicopter is far more critical than for an airplane. Some helicopters may be properly loaded for takeoff, but near the end of a long flight when the fuel tanks are almost empty, the CG may have shifted enough for the helicopter to be out of balance laterally or longitudinally. Before making any long flight, the CG with the fuel available for landing must be checked to ensure it is within the allowable range.

Airplanes with tandem seating normally have a limitation requiring solo flight to be made from the front seat in some airplanes or the rear seat in others. Some of the smaller helicopters also require solo flight be made from a specific seat, either the right, left, or center. These seating limitations are noted by a placard, usually on the instrument panel, and they should be strictly followed.

As an aircraft ages, its weight usually increases due to debris and dirt collecting in hard-to-reach locations and moisture absorbed in the cabin insulation. This increase in weight is normally small, but it can be determined only by accurately weighing the aircraft.

Changes of fixed equipment may have a major effect upon the weight of the aircraft. Many aircraft are overloaded by the installation of extra radios or instruments. Fortunately, the replacement of older, heavy electronic equipment with newer, lighter types results in a weight reduction. This weight change, however helpful, can cause the CG to shift, which must be computed and annotated in the weight and balance record.

Repairs and alterations are the major sources of weight changes. It is the responsibility of the FAA-certificated mechanic or repairman making any repair or alteration to know the weight and location of a change, to compute the CG, record the new empty weight and EWCG in the aircraft weight and balance record, and update the equipment lists.

If the newly calculated EWCG should happen to fall outside the EWCG range, it is necessary to perform an adverse-loading check. This requires a forward and rearward adverse-loading check and a maximum weight check. These weight and balance extreme conditions represent the maximum forward and rearward CG position for the aircraft. An adverse-loading check is a deliberate attempt to load an aircraft in a manner that creates the most critical balance condition and still remains within the design CG limits of the aircraft. If any of the checks fall outside the loaded CG range, the aircraft must be reconfigured or placarded to prevent the pilot from loading the aircraft improperly. It is sometimes possible to install a fixed ballast in order for the aircraft to operate again within the normal CG range.

The FAA-certificated mechanic or repairman conducting an annual or condition inspection must ensure the weight and balance data in the aircraft records is current and accurate. It is the responsibility of the PIC to use the most current weight and balance data when operating the aircraft.

Stability and Balance Control

Balance control refers to the location of the CG of an aircraft. This is of primary importance to aircraft stability, which is a factor in flight safety. The CG is the point at which the total weight of the aircraft is assumed to be concentrated, and the CG must be located within specific limits for safe flight. Both lateral and longitudinal balance are important, but the prime concern is longitudinal balance; that is, the location of the CG along the longitudinal or lengthwise axis.

An airplane is designed to have stability that allows it to be trimmed to maintain straight-and-level flight with hands off the controls. Longitudinal stability is maintained by ensuring the CG is slightly ahead of the center of lift. This produces a fixed nose-down force independent of the airspeed. This is balanced by a variable nose-up force, which is produced by a downward aerodynamic force on the horizontal tail surfaces

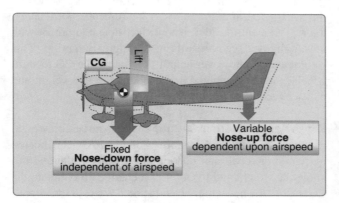

Figure 1-1. *Longitudinal forces acting on an airplane in flight.*

that varies directly with the airspeed. *[Figure 1-1]*
If a rising air current should cause the nose to pitch up, the airplane slows and the downward force on the tail decreases. The weight concentrated at the CG pulls the nose back down. If the nose should drop in flight, the airspeed increases and the increased downward tail load brings the nose back up to level flight.

As long as the CG is maintained within the allowable limits for its weight, the airplane has adequate longitudinal stability

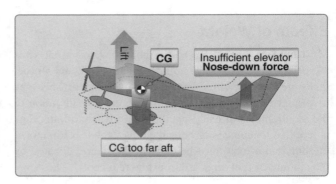

Figure 1-2. *If the CG is too far aft at the low stall airspeed, there might not be enough elevator nose-down authority to get the nose down for recovery.*

and control. If the CG is too far aft, it is too near the center of lift; the airplane is unstable and difficult to recover from a stall. *[Figure 1-2]* If the unstable airplane should enter a spin, the spin could become flat making recovery difficult or impossible. If the CG is too far forward, the downward tail load needs to be increased to maintain level flight. This increased tail load has the same effect as carrying additional weight; the aircraft must fly at a higher angle of attack and drag increases.

A more serious problem caused by the CG being too far forward is the lack of sufficient elevator authority. At low takeoff speeds, the elevator might not produce enough nose-up force to rotate; on landing there may not be enough elevator force to flare the airplane. *[Figure 1-3]* Both takeoff and landing runs are lengthened if the CG is too far forward. The basic aircraft design is such that lateral symmetry is assumed to exist. For each item of weight added to the left of the center line of the aircraft (also known as buttock line zero or BL-0), there is generally an equal weight at a corresponding location on the right.

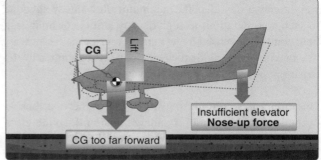

Figure 1-3. *If the CG is too far forward, there is not enough elevator nose-up force to flare the airplane for landing.*

The lateral balance can be upset by uneven fuel loading or burnoff. The position of the lateral CG is not normally computed for an airplane, but the pilot must be aware of the adverse effects that result from a laterally unbalanced condition. *[Figure 1-4]* This is corrected by using the aileron trim tab until enough fuel has been used from the tank on the heavy side to balance the airplane. The deflected trim tab deflects the aileron to produce additional lift on the heavy side, but it also produces additional drag, and the airplane flies inefficiently.

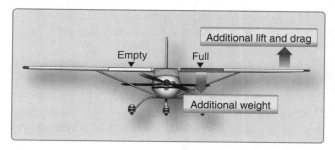

Figure 1-4. *Lateral imbalance causes wing heaviness, which may be corrected by deflecting the aileron. The additional lift causes additional drag, and the airplane flies inefficiently.*

Helicopters are more often affected by lateral imbalance than airplanes. If a helicopter is loaded with heavy occupants and fuel on the same side, it could be out of balance enough to make it unsafe to fly. It is also possible that if external loads are carried in such a position that requires large lateral displacement of the cyclic control to maintain level flight, the fore-and-aft cyclic control effectiveness is limited.

Swept-wing airplanes are more critical due to fuel imbalance because as the fuel is used from the outboard tanks, the CG shifts forward. As fuel is used from the inboard tanks, the CG shifts aft. *[Figure 1-5]* For this reason, fuel-use scheduling in swept-wing airplanes operation is critical.

Weight Control for Aircraft Other Than Fixed and Rotor-wing

Some light aircraft utilize different methods of determining weight and balance from the traditional fixed and rotor-wing aircraft. These aircraft achieve flight control by methods different from the fixed-wing airplane or helicopter. Most notable of these are weight-shift control (WSC) aircraft (also known as trikes), powered parachutes, and balloons. These aircraft typically do not specify either an EWCG or a CG range. They require only a certified or approved maximum weight. To understand why this is so, a look at how flight control is achieved is helpful.

Airplanes and WSC aircraft control flight under the influence of the same four forces (lift, gravity, thrust, and drag), and around the same three axes (pitch, yaw, and roll). However, each aircraft accomplishes this control in a very different manner. This difference helps explain why the fixed-wing

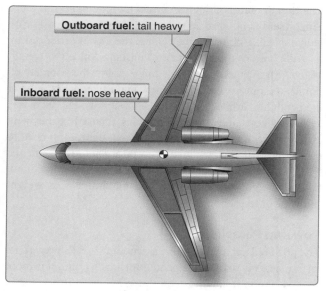

Figure 1-5. *Fuel in the tanks of a swept-wing airplane affects both lateral and longitudinal balance. As fuel is used from an outboard tank, the CG shifts forward.*

airplane requires an established weight and a known CG, whereas the WSC aircraft only requires the known weight.

The fixed-wing airplane has movable controls that alter lift on various airfoil surfaces to vary pitch, roll, and yaw. In turn, these changes in lift affect the characteristics of the flight parameters. Weight normally decreases in flight due to fuel consumption, and the airplane CG changes with this weight reduction. An airplane utilizes its variable flight controls to compensate and maintain controllability through the various flight modes and as the CG changes. An airplane has a CG range or envelope within which it must remain if the flight controls are to remain effective and the airplane safely operated.

Weight-Shift Control Aircraft

The WSC aircraft has a relatively set platform wing without a tail. The pilot achieves control by shifting weight. In the design of this aircraft, the weight of the airframe and its payload is attached to the wing at a single point in a pendulous arrangement. The pilot, through the flight controls, controls the arm of this pendulum and thereby controls the aircraft. When a change in flight parameter is desired, the pilot displaces the aircraft's weight by the appropriate distance and direction. This change momentarily disrupts the equilibrium between the four forces acting on the aircraft. The wing, due to its inherent stability, then moves appropriately to reestablish the desired relationship between these forces; the wing flexes and alters its shape. As the shape is changed, lift is varied at different points on the wing to achieve the desired flight parameters.

The flight controls primarily affect the pitch-and-roll axes. Since there is no vertical tail plane, there is minimal or no yaw control. Unlike in an airplane, the CG experienced by the WSC aircraft wing remains constant. Since the weight of the airframe acts through a single point (the wing attach point), the range over which the weight may act is fixed at the pendulum arm or length. Even though weight decreases as fuel is consumed, weight remains focused at the wing attach point. Because the range is fixed, there is no need to establish a calculated range. The pilot should consult the POH or Aircraft Operating Instructions (AOI) for maximum takeoff weight and minimum and maximum seat weight limits prior to each flight.

Powered Parachutes

The powered parachute is also a pendulum-style aircraft. Its airframe CG is fixed at the pendulum attach point. It is more limited in controllability than the WSC aircraft because it lacks an aerodynamic pitch control. Pitch (and lift) control is primarily a function of the power control. Increased power results in increased lift; cruise power amounts to level flight; decreased power causes a descent. Due to this characteristic, the aircraft is basically a one-airspeed aircraft. Once again, because the CG is fixed at the attach point to the wing, there is no CG range. As with WSC, the pilot should consult the POH or AOI for maximum takeoff weight and minimum and maximum seat weight limits prior to each flight.

Roll control on a powered parachute is achieved by changing the shape of the wing. The change is achieved by varying the length of steering lines attached to the outboard trailing edges of the wing. The trailing edge of the parachute is pulled down slightly on one side or the other to create increased drag along that side. This change in drag creates roll and yaw, permitting the aircraft to be steered.

Balloons

The balloon is controlled by the pilot only in the vertical dimension; this is in contrast to all other aircraft. He or she achieves this control through the use of lift and weight. Wind provides all other movement. The CG of the gondola remains constant beneath the balloon envelope. As in WSC and powered-parachute aircraft, there is no CG limitation.

Underestimating the Importance of Weight and Balance

Many pilots, from sport pilot to commercial pilot, tend to underestimate the importance of proper weight and balance of their aircraft. Load sheets are taken for granted and hasty calculations are made of the aircraft's CG. Unfortunately, each year there are a number of accidents related to weight and balance issues. Many of these occurrences could have been avoided had more attention been given to weight and balance.

Every student pilot is taught how to work a weight and balance problem and that it is important to make sure every flight is loaded "within the envelope" (no more than maximum gross weight) for both takeoff and landing. But does he or she really understand just why this is so and the disastrous effect of being out of the envelope? Two examples of documented cases are provided below in an effort to indicate the serious nature of maintaining the proper weight and balance. In case studies when weight and balance was listed as the major factor of the accident, many were fatal.

For instance, a small aircraft was loaded with hunters, gear, and dogs (none of the dogs were secured inside the aircraft). During takeoff, all the dogs went to the aft of the airplane. This shifted the CG well aft of its allowable limit. The airplane stalled and crashed. The airplane was destroyed with casualties.

Another accident occurred when a group of skydivers were sitting on the floor toward the aft portion of the airplane (they were unsecured). During takeoff, the CG was again well beyond its aft limit. The airplane stalled and crashed. The airplane was destroyed with casualties.

There is a safety factor built into the formula for maximum gross weight. Any airplane can fly when it takes off at a weight greater than maximum gross weight if the runway is long enough and the density altitude is low enough. However, landing is a different matter. All airplanes are built to withstand an occasional hard landing, but what would happen if the hard landing were combined with a substantially overweight airplane? Something would probably break at that time or the structure would be weakened enough to break sometime in the future when everything might seem normal to a pilot unaware of the previous situation. Even more disastrous than an overweight, hard landing is reaching or exceeding the structural integrity of the metal and/or composite design values when maneuvering or when turbulence is encountered. Hidden damage could result, causing an unexpected catastrophic failure at some future time.

If an airplane is certificated with a maximum gross weight of 6,000 pounds (its weight on the ground) and is rolled into a 60° bank, the forces exerted make it feel as if it weighed 12,000 pounds. At its maximum certificated gross weight, there is no problem because the aircraft is operated within its certificated maneuvering loads. But loaded to 8,000 pounds with a 60° bank or an abrupt pullup, it suddenly weighs 16,000 pounds and might not be able to perform! Even if it could, there would probably be internal stress damage that would show up on future flights.

Chapter 2

Weight and Balance Theory

Introduction

Weight and balance in aircraft is based on the law of the lever. This chapter discusses the application of the law of the lever and its applications relative to locating the balance point of a beam or lever on which various weights are located or shifted. The chapter also discusses the documentation pertaining to weight and balance that is furnished by the Federal Aviation Administration (FAA) and aircraft manufacturers.

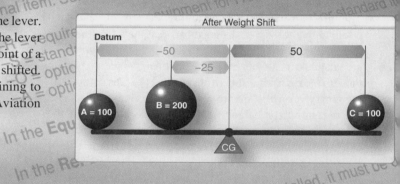

Item	Weight (lb)	Arm (in)	Moment	CG
Weight A	100	50	5,000	
Weight B	100	90	9,000	
Weight C	200	150	30,000	
	400		44,000	

em	Weight (lb) 2,300 max	Arm (in)	Moment	CG +35.6 to +43.2
plane	1,340	37	49,580	
nt seats	255	35	8,925	
ear seats	309	72	22,248	
Fuel	240	48	11,520	
Baggage	50	92	4,600	
			96,873	44.1

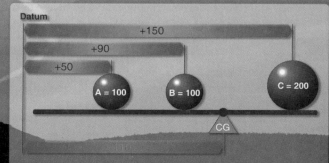

Weight and Balance Theory

Two elements are vital in the weight and balance considerations of an aircraft.

- The total weight of the aircraft must be no greater than the maximum weight allowed by the FAA for the make and model of the aircraft.

- The center of gravity (CG), or the point at which all of the weight of the aircraft is considered to be concentrated, must be maintained within the allowable range for the operational weight of the aircraft.

Arm

The arm is usually measured and expressed in inches and refers to the horizontal distance between the CG of an item or object and the datum, a point from where all measurements are taken. Arms to the left of the datum are negative (–) and those to the right of the datum are positive (+). The datum is an imaginary vertical plane from which all horizontal distances are measured for balance purposes. The position of the reference datum varies by aircraft design and manufacturer. When the datum is located off of the lever and to the left, all of the arms are positive and computational errors are minimized. Note: When the datum is established ahead of the aircraft, for example at the aircraft nose, all of the arms are positive and computational errors are minimized.

Moment

A moment is a force that tries to cause rotation and is the product of the arm, in inches, and the weight, in pounds. Moments are generally expressed in pound-inches (lb-in) and may be either positive or negative.

The Law of the Lever

Weight and balance problems are based on the physical law of the lever. This law states that a lever is balanced when the weight on one side of the fulcrum (a pivot point for the lever) multiplied by its arm is equal to the weight on the opposite side multiplied by its arm. In other words, the lever is balanced when the sum of the moments about the fulcrum is zero. This is the condition in which the positive moments (those that try to rotate the lever clockwise) are equal to the negative moments (those that try to rotate it counterclockwise). In an aircraft, the balance point is referred to as the CG.

One of the easiest ways to understand weight and balance is to consider a lever with weights placed at various locations. The balance point or CG of the lever can be changed by either moving the weights closer or farther from the fulcrum or by increasing or decreasing the weights. The balance point or CG of a lever may be determined by using these four steps:

1. Measure the arm of each weight in inches from the datum.

2. Multiply each arm by its weight in pounds to determine the moment in pound-inches of each weight.

3. Determine the total of all weights and of all the moments. (Disregard the weight of the lever).

4. Divide the total moment by the total weight to determine the balance point.

Consider these facts about the lever in *Figure 2-1*. The 100-pound weight A is located 50 inches to the left of the fulcrum (the datum, in this instance), and it has a moment of $100 \times -50 = -5,000$ lb-in. The 200-pound weight B is located 25 inches to the right of the fulcrum, and its moment is $200 \times +25 = +5,000$ lb-in. In *Figure 2-2*, the sum of the moments is $-5,000 + 5,000 = 0$, and the lever is balanced. The forces that try to rotate it clockwise have the same magnitude as those that try to rotate it counterclockwise. If either weight is moved or changed, the balance point or CG changes and the lever becomes unbalanced.

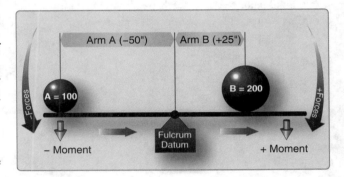

Figure 2-1. *Balance lever.*

Item	Weight (lb)	Arm (in)	Moment (lb-in)
Weight A	100	–50	–5,000
Weight B	200	+25	+5,000
	300		0

Figure 2-2. *Balance point locations.*

In *Figure 2-3*, the datum is located off the lever to the left of weight A. Using the information provided in *Figure 2-3*,

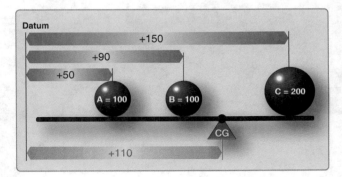

Figure 2-3. *Balance lever datum located off the lever.*

determine the balance point by making a chart like the one in *Figure 2-4*.

Item	Weight (lb)	Arm (in)	Moment	CG
Weight A	100	50	5,000	
Weight B	100	90	9,000	
Weight C	200	150	30,000	
	400		44,000	110

Figure 2-4. *Finding balance point with datum located off the lever.*

As noted in *Figure 2-4*, A weighs 100 pounds and is 50 inches from the datum; B weighs 100 pounds and is 90 inches from the datum; C weighs 200 pounds and is 150 inches from the datum. The total of the weights is 400 pounds, and the total moment is 44,000 lb-in.

Determine the balance point by dividing the total moment by the total weight. A balance point is equal to the CG and can be mathematically written as:

$$CG = \frac{\text{total moment}}{\text{total weight}}$$

To prove this is the correct balance, move the datum to a location 110 inches to the right of the original datum and determine the arm of each weight from this new datum. *[Figure 2-5]* Then, make a new chart similar to the one in *Figure 2-6*. If the balance point is correct, the sum of the moments is zero.

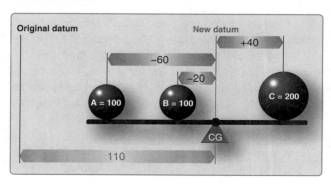

Figure 2-5. *Locating balance point.*

Item	Weight (lb)	Arm (in)	Moment (lb-in)
Weight A	100	−60	−6,000
Weight B	100	−20	−2,000
Weight C	200	+40	+8,000
			0

Figure 2-6. *Proving balance point with three weights is correct.*

The new arm of weight A is 60 inches (the difference between 110 and 50), and since this weight is to the left of the datum,

its arm is negative or −60 inches. The new arm of weight B is 20 inches (110 − 90), and it is also to the left of the datum, so it is −20; the new arm of weight C is 40 inches (150 − 110). It is to the right of the datum and is therefore positive.

The lever is balanced when the sum of the moments is zero. The location of the datum used for determining the arms of the weights is not important; it may be in various locations, but all of the measurements must be made from the same datum location.

The procedure for finding the balance point is the same anywhere the datum is located. In *Figure 2-7*, the datum is located at C. Weight A has an arm of −100 inches (negative because it is to the left) of the datum and weight B has an arm of −60 inches from the datum. The table in *Figure 2-8* is used to determine the new balance point.

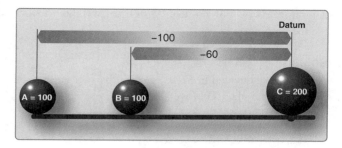

Figure 2-7. *Locating balance point with datum at C.*

Item	Weight (lb)	Arm (in)	Moment	CG
Weight A	100	−100	−10,000	
Weight B	100	−60	−6,000	
Weight C	200		0	
	400		−16,000	−40

Figure 2-8. *Determining new balance point.*

To verify that this is the correct balance point, move the datum 40 inches to the left of the original datum and determine the arm of each weight from this new datum as in *Figure 2-9*.

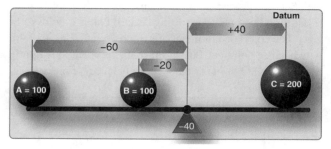

Figure 2-9. *Locating balance point with datum left of original.*

The new arm for weight A would be –100 + 40 = –60; for weight B, –60 + 40 = –20; and point C, is +40. The lever is balanced and the balance point is correct when the sum of the moments is zero. *[Figure 2-10]*

Item	Weight (lb)	Arm (in)	Moment (lb-in)
Weight A	100	–60	–6,000
Weight B	100	–20	–2,000
Weight C	200	40	+8,000
			0

Figure 2-10. *Proving the new balance point is correct.*

Shifting the Balance Point or CG

One common weight and balance problem involves moving or shifting weight from one point to another in order to move the balance point or CG to a desired location. This can be demonstrated by using a lever with three weights to work out the problem.

Solution by Chart

As the lever is loaded in *Figure 2-11*, it balances at a point 72 inches from the CG of weight A.

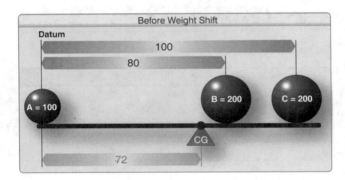

Figure 2-11. *Locating balance point with three weights.*

To shift weight B so the lever balances about its center, 50 inches from the CG of weight A, first determine the arm of weight B that produces a moment that causes the total moment of all three weights around this desired balance point to be zero. The combined moment of weights A and C around this new balance point is 5,000 lb-in, so the moment of weight B must be –5,000 lb-in for the lever to balance. *[Figure 2-12]*

Item	Weight (lb)	Arm (in)	Moment (lb-in)
Weight A	100	–50	–5,000
Weight B			
Weight C	200	+50	+10,000
			+5,000

Figure 2-12. *Proving the new balance point is correct.*

Determine the arm of weight B by dividing its moment, –5,000 lb-in, by its weight of 200 pounds. The arm is –25 inches. To balance the lever at its center, weight B must be placed so its CG is 25 inches to the left of the center of the lever. *[Figure 2-13]*

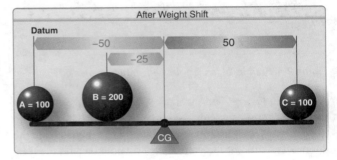

Figure 2-13. *Weight distribution to balance lever.*

Figure 2-14 indicates that the shift in weight depicted in *Figure 2-13* allows the lever to balance as the sum of the moments is zero.

Item	Weight (lb)	Arm (in)	Moment (lb-in)
Weight A	100	–50	–5,000
Weight B	200	–25	–5,000
Weight C	200	+50	+10,000
			0

Figure 2-14. *Weight shift provides correct CG.*

Basic Weight and Balance Equation

The following formulas can be used to determine the distance weight must be shifted to obtain a desired change in the CG location. The equation can also be rearranged to find the amount of weight required to be shifted to move the CG to a desired location, to find the distance the CG is moved when a specified amount of weight is shifted, or to find the total weight that would allow shifting a specified amount of weight to move the CG a given distance.

$$\frac{\text{Weight to be shifted}}{\text{Total weight}} = \frac{\Delta\,\text{CG}}{\text{Distance weight is shifted}}$$

$$\text{Total weight} = \frac{\text{Weight shifted} \times \text{Distance weight is shifted}}{\Delta\,\text{CG}}$$

$$\text{Weight shifted} = \frac{\text{Total weight shifted} \times \Delta\,\text{CG}}{\text{Distance weight is shifted}}$$

$$\Delta\,\text{CG} = \frac{\text{Weight shifted} \times \text{Distance weight is shifted}}{\text{Total weight}}$$

$$\text{Distance weight is shifted} = \frac{\text{Total weight} \times \Delta\,\text{CG}}{\text{Weight shifted}}$$

Solution by Formula

The problem in *Figure 2-11* can be solved by using variations of this basic equation. First, rearrange the formula to determine the distance weight B must be shifted:

$$\text{Distance weight B is shifted} = \frac{\text{Total weight} \times \Delta\,\text{CG}}{\text{Weight shifted}}$$

$$= \frac{500 \times -22}{200}$$

$$= -55 \text{ inches}$$

The CG of the lever in *Figure 2-11* was 72 inches from the datum. This CG can be shifted to the center of the lever as in *Figure 2-13* by moving weight B. If the 200-pound weight B is moved 55 inches to the left, the CG shifts from +72 inches to +50 inches, a distance of 22 inches.

When the distance the weight is to be shifted is known, the amount of weight to be shifted to move the CG to any location can be determined by another arrangement of the basic equation. Use the following arrangement of the formula to determine the amount of weight that has to be shifted from station 8 to station +25, to move the CG from station +72 to station +50.

$$\text{Weight shifted} = \frac{\text{Total weight} \times \Delta\,\text{CG}}{\text{Distance weight is shifted}}$$

$$= \frac{500 \times 22}{55}$$

$$= 200 \text{ inches}$$

If the 200-pound weight B is shifted from station +80 to station +25, the CG moves from station +72 to station +50.

A third arrangement of this basic equation is used to determine the amount the CG is shifted when a given amount of weight is moved for a specified distance (as it was done in *Figure 2-11*). The following formula is used to determine the amount the CG is shifted when 200-pound weight B is moved from +80 to +25.

$$\Delta\,\text{CG} = \frac{\text{Weight shifted} \times \text{Distance it is shifted}}{\text{Total weight}}$$

$$= \frac{200 \times 55}{500}$$

$$= 22 \text{ inches}$$

Moving weight B from +80 to +25 moves the CG 22 inches from its original location at +72 to its new location at +50 as seen in *Figure 2-13*.

To complete the calculations, return to the original formula and enter the appropriate numbers.

$$\frac{\text{Weight to be shifted}}{\text{Total weight}} = \frac{\Delta\,\text{CG}}{\text{Distance weight is shifted}}$$

$$\frac{200}{500} = \frac{22}{55}$$

$$.4 = .4$$

The equation is balanced.

Mean Aerodynamic Chord

The CG point affects the stability of the aircraft. To ensure the aircraft is safe to fly, the CG must fall within specified limits established by the manufacturer.

On some aircraft, the CG is expressed as a percentage of the length of the mean aerodynamic chord (MAC) or "percent MAC." *[Figure 2-14]* In order to make such a calculation, the position of the leading edge of the MAC must be known ahead of time.

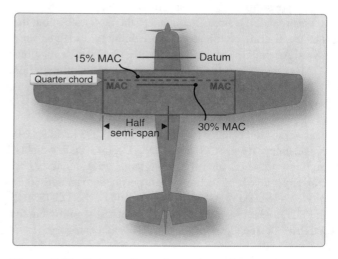

Figure 2-14. *Center of gravity expressed as percent mean aerodynamic chord.*

CG limits are specified forward and aft and/or lateral (left and right) limits within which the aircraft's CG must be located during flight. The area between the limits is called the CG range of the aircraft.

The position of the fore and aft CG limits is measured as a percentage of MAC from the MAC leading edge. Usually for a single or two-seat aircraft, the most forward position would be forward of 30–35 percent MAC. Thus, the allowable CG range in a light aircraft should not exceed 20 percent MAC.

Note: For a rectangular width of constant airfoil section dimensions, MAC is just the chord. For a symmetrically-tapered wing, it is the average of the root chord and the tip chord.

FAA-Furnished Weight and Balance Information

The information discussed to this point can be readily applied to any aircraft weight and balance problem. To apply the techniques, certain elements of information are required. This information is obtained from both FAA documents and manufacturer provided data.

Before an aircraft CG can be computed, certain information must be known. This information, furnished by the FAA for every certificated aircraft in the Type Certificate Data Sheets (TCDS) or Aircraft Specifications, can be accessed at www.faa.gov. When the design of an aircraft is approved by the FAA, an Approved Type Certificate and TCDS are issued. The TCDS includes all of the pertinent specifications for the aircraft; at each annual or 100-hour inspection, it is the responsibility of the inspecting mechanic or repairman to ensure that the aircraft adheres to them. A note about the TCDS: aircraft certificated before January 1, 1958, were issued Aircraft Specifications under the Civil Air Regulations (CARs), but when the Civil Aeronautical Administration (CAA) was replaced by the FAA, Aircraft Specifications were replaced by the TCDS.

The weight and balance information on a TCDS includes CG range, empty weight CG range (EWCG), maximum weights, number of seats, maximum baggage, fuel capacity, oil capacity, and datum location. Data pertinent to an individual model is located in its respective section of the TCDS. Use the TCDS excerpts in *Figure 2-15* to verify the following for a Cirrus Design Corporation SR 20 normal category:

CG Range
S/N 1005 through 1147:

Forward Limits: 138.7 inches at 2,110 lb with a straight line taper to 141.0 in at 2,694 lb and 143.0 in at 2,900 lb

Aft Limits: 144.6 in at 2,110 lb, with straight line taper to 147.4 in at 2,570 lb, and to 147.9 in at 2,745 lb, and 148.2 in at 2,900 lb

S/N 1148 through 1877, 1879 through 1885, and S/N 1005 through 1147 if Cirrus Service Bulletin SB 20-01-00 is complied with:

Forward Limits: 138.7 in at 2,110 lb with a straight line taper to 141.0 in at 2,694 lb and 144.1 in at 3,000 lb

Aft Limits: 144.6 in at 2,110 lb, with straight line taper to 147.4 in at 2,570 lb, and to 148.1 in at 2,900 lb, and 148.0 in at 3,000 lb

S/N 1878, 1886 and Subsequent:

Forward Limits: 137.8 in at 2,100 lb with a straight line taper to 139.1 in at 2,700 lb, and to 140.7 in at 3,050 lb

Aft Limits: 148.1 in at 2,100 lb, with straight line to 148.1 in at 3,050 lb

Empty Weight CG Range (EWCG)

When all of the seats and baggage compartments are located close together, it is not possible (as long as the EWCG is located within the EWCG range) to legally load the aircraft so that its operational CG falls outside this allowable range. If the seats and baggage areas extend over a wide range, the EWCG range is listed as "None."

Maximum Weights

The maximum allowable takeoff and landing weights and the maximum allowable ramp weight are given. This basic information may be altered by a note. Notes are found in data pertinent to all models. An example would be Note 6 at the end of *Figure 2-15*.

Number of Seats

The number of seats and their arms are given in such terms as: 4 (2 at 143.5 aft of datum, 2 at 180 aft of datum).

Maximum Baggage

Maximum baggage for this model is 130 pounds at 208 inches.

Fuel Capacity

This important information is given in such terms as: 60.5 gal at 153.75 in. Usable: 56 gal (See Note 1). Notes can be found in data pertinent to all models.

Oil Capacity (Wet Sump)

The quantity of the full oil supply and its arm are given: 8 quarts at 76.2 in.

| A00009CH |
| Revision 16 |
| Cirrus Design Corporation |
| SR20 |
| SR22 |
| April 22, 2009 |

TYPE CERTIFICATE DATA SHEET NO. A00009CH

This data sheet, which is part of Type Certificate No. A00009CH, prescribes conditions and limitations under which the product for the which type certificate was issued meets the airworthiness requirements of the Federal Aviation Regulations.

Type Certificate Holder: Cirrus Design Corporation
4515 Taylor Circle
Duluth, MN 55811

I - Model SR20, (Normal Category), Approved October 23, 1998

Engine   Teledyne Continental IO-360-ES, Type Certificate Data Sheet (TCDS) E1CE

Fuel   100/100LL minimum grade aviation gasoline

Engine Limits   Maximum Take-off   2700 RPM (200 hp)
                Maximum Continuous Power 2700 RPM (200 hp)

Propeller and
Propeller limits

1. Hartzell Propeller Inc. P/N BHC-J2YF-1BF/F7694
TCDS P37EA
Maximum Diameter: 76 inches
Minimum Diameter: 73 inches
Number of Blades: 2
Low Pitch: 14.6°+/-0.5°
High Pitch: 35.0°+/-1.0°
Not to be operated above 24 inches of manifold pressure between 1900 and 2200 RPM.
Spinner: Hartzell P/N A-2295(P) NOTE: Spinner may be painted or polished.

2. Hartzell Propeller Inc. P/N PHC-J3YF-1MF/F7392-1
TCDS P36EA
Maximum Diameter: 74 inches
Minimum Diameter: 72 inches
Number of Blades: 3
Low Pitch: 14.1°+/-0.5°
High Pitch: 35.0°+/-1.0°
No operating limitations to 2800 RPM
Spinner: Hartzell P/N A-2295-1P

3. Hartzell Propeller Inc. P/N PHC-J3YF-1RF/F7392-1
TCDS P36EA
Maximum Diameter: 74 inches
Minimum Diameter: 72 inches
Number of Blades: 3
Low Pitch: 13.9°+/-0.5°
High Pitch: 35.0°+/-1.0°
No operating limitations to 2800 RPM
Spinner: Hartzell P/N A-2295-1(P) NOTE: Spinner may be painted or polished.

Page No.	1	2	3	4	5	6	7
Rev. No.	11	12	12	14	14	16	16

Figure 2-15. *Sample excerpt from TCDS A00009CH.*

Airspeed Limits

S/N 1005 thru 1147:

V_{ne}	Never Exceed Speed	200 KIAS
V_{no}	Maximum Structural Cruising Speed	165 KIAS
V_o	(2900 lbs) Operating Maneuvering Speed	135 KIAS
Vo	(2600 lbs) Operating Maneuvering Speed	126 KIAS
Vo	(2200 lbs) Operating Maneuvering Speed	116 KIAS
V_{fe}	Maximum Flap Extension Speed	100 KIAS
V_{pd}	Maximum Parachute Deployment Speed	135 KIAS

S/N 1148 thru 1877, 1879 thru 1885, and S/N 1005 thru 1147 if Cirrus Service Bulletin SB 20-01-00 is complied with:

V_{ne}	Never Exceed Speed	200 KIAS
V_{no}	Maximum Structural Cruising Speed	165 KIAS
V_o	(3000 lbs) Operating Maneuvering Speed	131 KIAS
Vo	(2600 lbs) Operating Maneuvering Speed	122 KIAS
Vo	(2300 lbs) Operating Maneuvering Speed	114 KIAS
V_{fe}	Maximum Flap Extension Speed	100 KIAS
V_{pd}	Maximum Parachute Deployment Speed	135 KIAS

S/N 1878, 1886 and subsequent:

Vne	Never Exceed Speed	200 KIAS
Vno	Maximum Structural Cruising Speed	163 KIAS
Vo	(3050 lbs) Operating Maneuvering Speed	130 KIAS
Vfe	Maximum Flap Extension Speed	104 KIAS
Vpd	Maximum Parachute Deployment Speed	133 KIAS

C.G. Range

S/N 1005 thru 1147:
Forward Limits: 138.7 inches at 2110 lbs with a straight line taper to 141.0 inches at 2694 lbs, and 143.0 inches at 2900 lbs.

Aft Limits: 144.6 inches at 2110 lbs, with straight line taper to 147.4 inches at 2570 lbs, and to 147.9 inches at 2745 lbs, and 148.2 inches at 2900 lbs.

S/N 1148 thru 1877, 1879 thru 1885, and S/N 1005 thru 1147 if Cirrus Service Bulletin SB 20-01-00 is complied with:
Forward Limits: 138.7 inches at 2110 lbs with a straight line taper to 141.0 inches at 2694 lbs, and 144.1 inches at 3000 lbs.

Aft Limits: 144.6 inches at 2110 lbs, with straight line taper to 147.4 inches at 2570 lbs, and to 148.1 inches at 2900 lbs, and 148.0 inches at 3000 lbs.

S/N 1878, 1886 and subsequent:
Forward Limits: 137.8 inches at 2100 lbs with a straight line taper to 139.1 inches at 2700 lbs, and to 140.7 inches at 3050 lbs

Aft Limits: 148.1 inches at 2100 lbs, with straight line to 148.1 inches at 3050 lbs.

Empty Weight
C.G. Range

None

Maximum Weight

S/N 1005 thru 1147:
Takeoff and Landing: 2900 lbs.

S/N 1148 thru 1877, 1879 thru 1885, and S/N 1005 thru 1147 if Cirrus Service Bulletin SB 20-01-00 is complied with:

Takeoff:	3000 lbs.
Landing:	2900 lbs.
Zero Fuel:	2900 lbs.

S/N 1878, 1886 and subsequent:
Takeoff and Landing: 3050 lbs.

Figure 2-15. *Sample excerpt from TCDS A00009CH (continued).*

Minimum Crew	One (1) Pilot
Number of Seats	4 (2 at 143.5 inches aft of datum, 2 at 180 inches aft of datum)
Maximum Baggage	130 Lbs. at 208 inches
Fuel Capacity Total:	S/N 1005 thru 1877, 1879 thru 1885 60.5 gal at 153.75 inches Usable: 56 gal (See Note 1) S/N 1878, 1886 and subsequent: 58.5 gal at 154.9 inches Usable: 56 gal (See Note 1)
Oil Capacity	8 quarts at 76.2 inches
Maximum Operating Altitude	With a portable oxygen system, the aircraft is limited to 17,500 ft MSL. Oxygen must be provided as required by the operating rules. Only portable oxygen systems listed in the FAA Approved Airplane Flight Manual, document number 11934-002, or later FAA approved revisions, are allowed.

Control Surface Movements

Wing Flaps:	Up 0°± 0.5°	Down 50% 16°± 0.5° Down 100% 32°± 0.5°
Aileron:	Up 12.5° ± 1.0°	Down 12.5° ±1.0°
Elevator:	Up 25.0° +0°/-1.0°	Down 15° ± 1.0°
Elevator Trim:	Up 17.0° Minimum	Down 10.5° ± 1.0°
Rudder:	Right 20.0° ± 1.0°	Left 20.0° ± 1.0°

Additional Limitations:	Airframe life limit: 12,000 flight hours
Design Data:	The airplane shall be manufactured in accordance with the latest FAA approved revision of "Master Drawing List", Document No. 13750, or other FAA approved data. NOTE: Document No. 12609 is the predecessor document to Document No. 13750.
Serial Nos. Eligible	1005 and on

Figure 2-15. *Sample excerpt from TCDS A00009CH (continued).*

Data Pertinent to All Models

Reference Datum	100 inches in front of the forward face of firewall bulkhead
Leveling Means	Door sill and leveling points as defined in AFM
Certification Basis	Model SR20: 14 CFR Part 23 of the Federal Aviation Regulations effective February 1, 1965, as amended by 23-1 through 23-47, except as follows:

14 CFR 23.573, 23.575, 23.611, 23.657, 23.673 through Amendment 23-48;

14 CFR 23.783, 23.785, 23.867, 23.1303, 23.1307, 23.1309, 23.1311, 23.1321, 23.1323, 23.1329, 23,1361, 23.1383, 23.1401, 23.1431, 23.1435 through Amendment 23-49;

14 CFR 23.3, 23.25, 23.143, 23.145, 23.155, 23.1325, 23.1521, 23.1543, 23.1555, 23.1559, 23.1567, 23.1583, 23.1585, 23.1589 through Amendment 23-50;

14 CFR 23.777, 23.779, 23.901, 23.907, 23.955, 23.959, 23.963, 23.965, 23.973, 23.975, 23.1041, 23.1091, 23.1093, 23.1107, 23.1121, 23.1141, 23.1143, 23.1181, 23.1191, 23.1337 through Amendment 23-51;

14 CFR 23.1305 through Amendment 23-52

Noise: 14 CFR Part 36 dated December 1, 1969 as amended by 36-1 through 36-21.

Figure 2-15. *Sample excerpt from TCDS A00009CH (continued).*

Note 3.	FAA approved Airworthiness Limitations are included in Section 4 of the Airplane Maintenance Manual (AMM) Document No. 12137-001 for model SR20, and 13773-001 for model SR22.
Note 4.	Exterior colors are limited to those specified in the latest FAA accepted revision of the Airplane Maintenance Manual (AMM) Document No. 12137-001 for model SR20, and 13773-001 for model SR22.
Note 5.	Major structural repairs must be accomplished in accordance with FAA approved Cirrus Design repair methods or other methods approved by the FAA.
Note 6.	For Model SR22 S/N 0002 thru 2333, 2335 thru 2419, and 2421 thru 2437 a maximum landing weight exists along the line between 141.4 inches at 3210 lbs and 142.7 inches at 3400 lbs.

Figure 2-15. *Sample excerpt from TCDS A00009CH (continued).*

Data Pertinent to all Models

The location of the datum is specified and is described, for example, as: 100 inches in front of the forward face of the firewall bulkhead.

Manufacturer-Furnished Information

When an aircraft is initially certificated, its empty weight and EWCG are determined and recorded in the weight and balance record, such as the one in *Figure 2-16*. Notice in this figure that the moment is expressed as "Moment (lb-in/1,000)." This is a moment index, which means that the moment, a very large number, has been divided by 1,000 to make it more manageable. Chapter 4, Light Sport Aircraft—Weight and Balance Control, discusses moment indices in more detail.

The aircraft is furnished with an equipment list, specifies all the required equipment and all equipment approved for installation in the aircraft. The weight and arm of all installed equipment are included on the list and checked prior to the aircraft leaving the factory.

When an aircraft mechanic or repairman adds or removes any item on the equipment list, he or she must change the weight and balance record to indicate the new empty weight and EWCG, and the equipment list is revised to show which equipment is actually installed. *Figure 2-17* is from a comprehensive equipment list that includes all of the items of equipment approved for this particular model of aircraft. The pilot's operating handbook (POH) for each individual aircraft includes an aircraft-specific equipment list of the items from this master list. When any item is added to or removed from the aircraft, its weight and arm are determined in the equipment list and used to update the weight and balance record. The POH and airplane flight manual (AFM) also contain CG moment envelopes and loading graphs. Examples of the use of these helpful graphs are given in Chapter 5, Single-Engine Aircraft Weight and Balance Computations.

In addition to the weight and balance report and equipment list, the manufacturer also provides a CG range chart. The CG range can be found in text form in the TCDS. The CG range chart is furnished in the POH.

Aircraft Serial No. 18259080		FAA Registration No. N42565		Date: 4-22-09
Item	Weight (lb) x	C.G. Arm (in)	Moment (lb-in/1,000)	
Standard empty weight	1,876.0	36.1	67,798.6	
Optional equipment	1.2	13.9	16.7	
Special installation	6.2	41.5	257.3	
Paint	—	—	—	
Unusable fuel	30.0	46.0	1,380.0	
Basic empty weight	1,913.4		69,452.6	

Figure 2-16. *Weight and balance report.*

Comprehensive Equipment List

This is a comprehensive list of all Cessna equipment which is available for the Model 182S airplane. It should not be confused with the airplane-specific equipment list. An airplane-specific list is provided with each individual airplane at delivery, and is typically inserted at the rear of this Pilot's Operating Handbook. The following comprehensive equipment list and the airplane-specific list have a similar order of listing.

The comprehensive equipment list provides the following information in column form:

In the **Item No** column, each item is assigned a coded number. The first two digits of the code represent the assignment of item within the ATA Specification 100 breakdown (Chapter 11 for Placards, Chapter 21 for Air Conditioning, Chapter 77 for Engine Indicating, etc...). These assignments also correspond to the Maintenance Manual chapter breakdown for the airplane. After the first two digits (and hyphen), items receive a unique sequence number (01, 02, 03, etc...). After the sequence number (and hyphen), a suffix letter is assigned to identify equipment as a required item, a standard item or an optional item. Suffix letters are as follows:

  −R = required items or equipment for FAA certification
  −S = standard equipment items
  −O = optional equipment items replacing required or standard items
  −A = optional equipment items which are in addition to required or standard items

In the **Equipment List Description** column, each item is assigned a descriptive name to help identify its function.

In the **Ref Drawing** column, a drawing number is provided which corresponds to the item.

Note

If additional equipment is to be installed, it must be done in accordance with the reference drawing, service bulletin or a separate FAA approval.

In the **Wt Lbs** and **Arm Ins** columns, information is provided on the weight (in pounds) and arm (in inches) of the equipment item.

Notes

Unless otherwise indicated, true values (not net change values) for the weight and arm are shown. Positive arms are distances aft of the airplane datum; negative arms are distances forward of the datum.

Asterisks (*) in the weight and arm column indicate complete assembly installations. Some major components of the assembly are listed on the lines immediately following. The sum of these major components does not necessarily equal the complete assembly installation.

Figure 2-17. *Excerpt from a typical comprehensive equipment list.*

Item No	Equipment List Description	Ref Drawing	Wt (lbs.)	Arm (ins.)
24-04-S	Basic Avionics Kit Installation		4.3*	55.5*
	- Support Straps Installation		0.1	10.0
	- Avionics Cooling Fan Installation		1.6	3.0
	- Avionics Ground Installations		0.1	41.0
	- Circuit Breaker Panel Installation		1.5	16.5
	- Microphone Installation		0.2	18.5
	- Omni Antenna Installation		0.5	252.1
	- Omni Antenna Cable Assembly Installation		0.3	248.0
	Chapter 25 – Equipment/Furnishings			
25-01-R	Seat, Pilot, Adjustable		33.8	41.5
25-02-S	Seat, Copilot, Adjustable		33.8	41.5
25-03-S	Seat, Rear, Two Piece Back Cushion		50.0	82.0
25-04-R	Seat Belt and Shoulder Harness, Inertia Reel, Pilot and Copilot		5.2	50.3
25-05-S	Seat Belt and Shoulder Harness, Inertia Reel, Rear Seat		5.2	87.8
25-06-S	Sun Visors (Set of 2)		1.2	33.0
25-07-S	Baggage Retaining Net		0.5	108.0
25-08-S	Cargo Tie Down Rings (10 Tie Downs)		0.4	108.0
25-09-S	Pilot's Operating Checklist (Stowed in Instrument Panel Map Case)		0.3	15.0
25-10-R	Pilot's Operating Handbook and FAA Approved Airplane Flight Manual (Stowed in Pilot's Seat Back)		1.2	61.5
25-11-S	Fuel Sampling Cup		0.1	14.3
25-12-S	Tow Bar, Nose Gear (Stowed)		1.7	108.0
25-13-S	Emergency Locator Transmitter Installation		2.2*	134.8*
	- ELT Transmitter		1.7	135.0
	- Antenna and Cable Assembly		0.4	133.0
	- Hardware		0.1	138.0
	Chapter 26 – Fire Protection			
26-01-S	Fire Extinguisher Installation		5.3*	29.0*
	- Fire Extinguisher		4.8	29.0
	- Mounting Clamp & Hardware		0.5	29.0
	Chapter 27 – Flight Controls			
27-01-S	Dual Controls Installation, Right Seat		6.3*	12.9*
	- Control Wheel, Copilot		2.0	26.0
	- Rudder and Brake Pedal Installation Copilot		4.3	6.8

Figure 2-17. *Excerpt from a typical comprehensive equipment list (continued).*

Chapter 3

Weighing the Aircraft and Determining the Empty Weight Center of Gravity

Datum

LEMA

CG   MAC

TEMA

Introduction

Chapter 2, Weight and Balance Theory, explained the theory of weight and balance and gave examples of the way the center of gravity (CG) could be found for a lever loaded with several weights. In this chapter, the practical aspects of weighing an airplane and locating its CG are discussed. Formulas are introduced that allow the CG location to be measured in inches from various datum locations and in percentage of the mean aerodynamic chord (MAC).

R22

Datum

153

88.2

D = 75

L = 78.0

$$\text{CG inches from datum} = \text{LEMAC} + \frac{\text{MAC} \times \text{CG \% MAC}}{100}$$

$$= 144 + \frac{62 \times 27.4}{100}$$

$$= 160.9$$

$$\text{CG} = \frac{\text{Total moment}}{\text{Total weight}}$$

$$= \frac{65,756}{2,006}$$

$$= 32.8 \text{ inches behind the datum}$$

Weighing point	Scale reading (lb)	Net weight (lb)	Net weight (lb)	Arm (inches)	Moment (lb-in)	CG
Right side	846	16	830	46.0	38,180	
Left side	852	16	836	46.0	38,456	
Nose	348	8	340	−32.0	−10,880	
Total			2,006		65,756	32.8

Requirements

Regulations do not require periodic weighing of privately owned and operated aircraft. Such aircraft are usually weighed when originally certificated or after major alterations that can affect the weight and balance. The primary purpose of aircraft weight and balance control is safety. Manufacturers conduct extensive flight tests to establish loading limits for their aircraft because limit information is critical for safe flight. A secondary purpose is to aid efficiency during flight. Overloading of the aircraft is not the only concern; the distribution of the weight is important also. The aircraft has CG limits, and any loading that places the CG outside the established limits seriously impairs controllability of the aircraft.

Weight and balance is of such vital importance that each Federal Aviation Administration (FAA) certificated mechanic or repairman maintaining an aircraft must be fully aware of his or her responsibility to provide the pilot with current and accurate information for the actual weight of the aircraft and the location of the CG. The pilot in command (PIC) is responsible for knowing the weight of the load, CG, maximum allowable weight, and CG limits of the aircraft. The weight and balance report must include an equipment list showing weights and moment arms of all required and optional items of equipment included in the certificated empty weight.

Weight and balance records used in accounting for and correcting the CG location are reliable for only limited periods of time. For this reason, periodic aircraft weighing is desirable. An aircraft should be reweighed and a new weight and balance record should be started after the aircraft has undergone extensive repair or major alteration, when the pilot reports unsatisfactory flight characteristics (e.g., nose or tail heaviness), and when recorded weight and balance data are suspected to be in error.

Repairs and alterations are major sources of weight change. The airframe and powerplant (A&P) FAA-certificated mechanic or repairman who is responsible for making any repair or alteration must:

1. Establish by computation that the authorized weight and CG limits as shown in the type certificate data sheet (TCDS) and aircraft specifications are not exceeded, and

2. Record the new empty weight center of gravity (EWCG) data in the current approved aircraft flight manual or issued operating limitations.

When an aircraft has undergone extensive repair or major alteration, it should be reweighed and a new weight and balance record started. The A&P FAA-certificated mechanic or repairman responsible for the work must provide the pilot with current and accurate aircraft weight information and location of the EWCG.

Equipment for Weighing

Weighing aircraft with accurately calibrated scales is the only sure method of obtaining an accurate empty weight and CG location. The two basic types of scales used to weigh aircraft are platform and load cell.

Platform scales *[Figure 3-1]* or ramp wheel scales *[Figure 3-2]* (usually a form or modified version of the platform scale) are low profile, easy to handle, safe, and reliable. Tow or push the aircraft wheels or skids onto the scale pad at ground level. With one scale per wheel, each device should be capable of measuring up to at least 60,000 pounds since the weight on each wheel rarely exceeds this figure.

Figure 3-1. *Platform scales.*

Load cell scales [Figure 3-3] are also a reliable means to weigh aircraft and are typically cheaper than the platform type.Using load cell scales allows for the aircraft to be set up and weighed in its level flight attitude. With this method, the aircraft is placed on jacks with electronic load cells placed between the jack and the jack pad on the aircraft. The aircraft is raised on the jacks until the wheels or skids are off the floor and the aircraft is in a level flight attitude. The weight measured by each load cell is indicated on the control panel. Jacking an aircraft off the ground from all load points can be an inconvenience, as well as a safety risk, which some operators would rather avoid by opting for more expensive—but simpler to use—platform equipment. In addition, weighing with platform scales typically takes only one-third of the time needed to weigh with load cells.

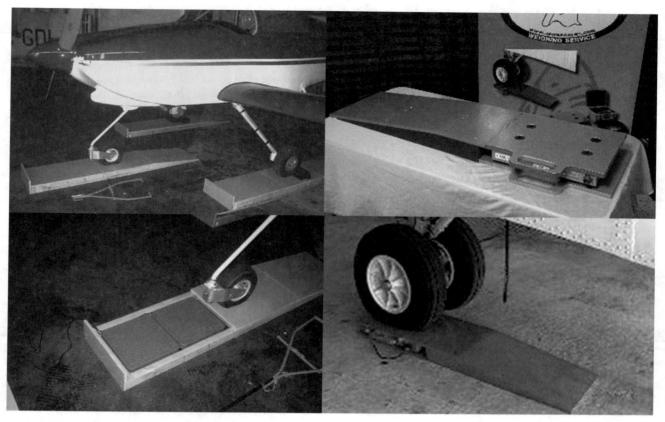

Figure 3-2. *Ramp scales.*

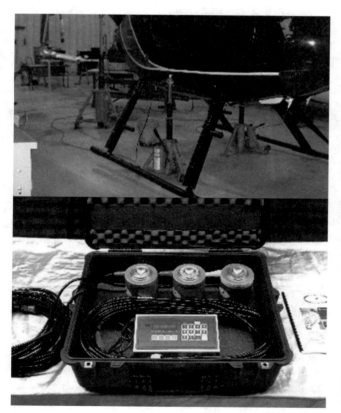

Figure 3-3. *Load cell scales.*

All scales for aviation use, manual or electronic, must be protected when stored or shipped, and they must be checked periodically for accuracy. The maximum recognized period between calibration checks is 12 months; however, this period may be reduced by an airworthiness authority dependent on the conditions of use. Scales in daily use may require a shorter interval and/or testing to determine the continued accuracy of the unit. Scales should be returned to the manufacturer for proper calibration and testing.

Preparation for Weighing

In general, weight procedures may vary with the aircraft and types of weight equipment employed. The weighing procedure contained in the manufacturer's maintenance manual should be followed for each particular aircraft. The major considerations in preparing an aircraft for weighing are described in the following paragraphs.

Scale Preparation

Mechanical and electronic scales shall be inspected prior to use and set to zero. This is done by adding and removing a weight, then rechecking for zero. This process should be repeated until a steady zero setting is obtained. The scales should be located in the same environment in which they are to be used and allowed to come up to temperature at least 2 hours prior to use. Scales should not be used in temperature extremes below 40 °F or above 100 °F unless the scale is specifically designed for use in those temperatures. Electronic scales are very sensitive and, if subjected to freezing temperatures, the liquid displays may be damaged beyond use.

Weigh Clean Aircraft Inside Hangar

The aircraft should be weighed inside a hangar where wind cannot blow over the surface and cause fluctuating or false scale readings. The aircraft should be clean inside and out, with special attention paid to the bilge area to ensure that no water or debris is trapped there. The outside of the aircraft should be as free as possible of all mud and dirt.

Equipment List

All of the required equipment must be properly installed, and there should be no equipment installed that is not included in the equipment list. If such equipment is installed, the weight and balance record must be corrected to indicate it.

Ballast

All required permanent ballasts must be properly secured in place. All temporary ballasts must be removed.

Standard Weights

Standard weights are established weights for numerous items involved in weight and balance computations. These weights should not be used if actual weights are available. Some of the standard weights are listed in *Figure 3-4*.

Weighing Point	Pounds per U.S. Gallon	
	32 °F	59 °F
AVGAS (Aviation Gasoline)	6.14	6.01
JET A & A-1	6.75	6.68
Water	8.35	8.33
Oil	7.50	7.43

Figure 3-4. *Standard fuels and weights with temperatures of 32 °F and 59 °F.*

Note the difference in weight as temperatures change. Although this change is a very small amount per gallon, it could end up in a significant total weight gain when dealing with large quantities of fluids, such as those found in commercial aircraft.

Draining the Fuel

Drain fuel from the tanks in the manner specified by the aircraft manufacturer. If there are no specific instructions, drain the fuel until the fuel quantity gauges read empty when the aircraft is in level-flight attitude. Any fuel remaining in the system is considered residual or unusable fuel and is part of the aircraft empty weight.

The amount of residual fuel and its arm are normally found in Note 1 in the section of the Type Certificate Data Sheets (TCDS), "Data pertaining to all Models." For additional fuel capacity information, see Chapter 2, Weight and Balance Theory.

If it is not feasible to drain the fuel, the tanks can be topped off to be sure of the quantity they contain and the aircraft weighed with full fuel. After weighing is complete, the weight of the fuel and its moment are subtracted from those of the aircraft as weighed. To correct the empty weight for the residual fuel, add its weight and moment.

When computing the weight of the fuel (e.g., a tank full of jet fuel), measure its specific gravity (sg) with a hydrometer and multiply it by 8.345 (the nominal weight of 1 gallon of pure water whose sg is 1.0). If the ambient temperature is high and the jet fuel in the tank is hot enough for its specific gravity to reach 0.81 rather than its nominal sg of 0.82, the fuel actually weighs 6.76 pounds per gallon rather than its normal weight of 6.84 pounds per gallon.

Oil

The empty weight for aircraft certificated under the Civilian Air Regulations (CAR) part 3 does not include the engine lubricating oil. The oil must either be drained before the aircraft is weighed, or its weight must be subtracted from the scale readings to determine the empty weight. To weigh an aircraft that does not include the engine lubricating oil as part of the empty weight, place it in level flight attitude, then open the drain valves and allow the oil to drain out. Any remaining is undrainable oil and is part of the empty weight. Aircraft certificated under Title 14 of the Code of Federal Regulations (14 CFR) parts 23 and 25 include full oil as part of the empty weight. If it is impractical to drain the oil, the reservoir can be filled to the specified level and the weight of the oil computed at 7.5 pounds per gallon. Then, its weight and moment are subtracted from the weight and moment of the aircraft as weighed. The amount and arm of the undrainable oil are found in Note 1 of the TCDS, and this must be added to the empty weight.

Other Fluids

The hydraulic fluid reservoir and all other reservoirs containing fluids required for normal operation of the aircraft should be full. Fluids not considered to be part of the empty weight of the aircraft are potable (drinkable) water, lavatory precharge water, and water for injection into the engines.

Configuration of the Aircraft

Consult the aircraft service manual regarding position of the landing gear shock struts and the control surfaces for weighing. When weighing a helicopter, the main rotor must be in its correct position.

Jacking the Aircraft

Aircraft are often weighed by rolling them onto ramps in which load cells are embedded. This eliminates the problems associated with jacking the aircraft off the ground. However, many aircraft are weighed by jacking the aircraft up and then lowering them onto scales or load cells.

Extra care must be used when raising an aircraft on jacks for weighing. If the aircraft has spring steel landing gear and it is jacked at the wheel, the landing gear will slide inward as the weight is taken off of the tire, and care must be taken to prevent the jack from tipping over.

For some aircraft, stress panels or plates must be installed before the aircraft is raised with wing jacks to distribute the weight over the jack pad. Be sure to follow the recommendations of the aircraft manufacturer in detail anytime an aircraft is jacked. When using two wing jacks, take special care to raise them simultaneously, keeping the aircraft so it does not slip off the jacks. As the jacks are raised, keep the safety collars screwed down against the jack cylinder to prevent the aircraft from tilting if one of the jacks should lose hydraulic pressure.

Leveling the Aircraft

When an aircraft is weighed, it must be in its level flight attitude so that all of the components are at their correct distance from the datum. This attitude is determined by information in the TCDS. Some aircraft require a plumb line to be dropped from a specified location so that the point of the weight (the bob) hangs directly above an identifiable point. Others specify that a spirit level be placed across two leveling lugs, often special screws on the outside of the fuselage. Other aircraft call for a spirit level to be placed on the upper door sill.

Lateral level is not specified for all light aircraft, but provisions are normally made on helicopters for determining both longitudinal and lateral level. This may be done by built-in leveling indicators, or by a plumb bob that shows the conditions of both longitudinal and lateral level.

The actual adjustments to level the aircraft using load cells are made with the jacks. When weighing from the wheels, leveling is normally done by adjusting the air pressure in the nosewheel shock strut.

Safety Considerations

Special precautions must be taken when raising an aircraft on jacks.

1. Stress plates must be installed under the jack pads if the manufacturer specifies them.

2. If anyone is required to be in the aircraft while it is being jacked, there must be no movement.

3. The jacks must be straight under the jack pads before beginning to raise the aircraft.

4. All jacks must be raised simultaneously and the safety devices are against the jack cylinder to prevent the aircraft tipping if any jack should lose pressure. Not all jacks have screw down collars, some use drop pins or friction locks.

Determining the CG

When the aircraft is in its level flight attitude, drop a plumb line from the datum and make a mark on the hangar floor below the tip of the bob. Draw a chalk line through this point parallel to the longitudinal axis of the aircraft.

Then, draw lateral lines between the actual weighing points for the main wheels, and make a mark along the longitudinal line at the weighing point for the nosewheel or the tailwheel. These lines and marks on the floor allow accurate measurements between the datum and the weighting points to determine their arms.

Determine the CG by adding the weight and moment of each weighing point to determine the total weight and total moment. Then, divide the total moment by the total weight to determine the CG relative to the datum. As an example of locating the CG with respect to the datum, which in this case is the firewall, consider the tricycle landing gear airplane as detailed in the *Figure 3-5* table and illustrated in *Figure 3-6*.

When the airplane is on the scales with the parking brakes

Weighing point	Scale reading (lb)	TARE weight (lb)	Net weight (lb)	Arm (in)	Moment (lb-in)	CG
Right side	846	16	830	46.0	38,180	
Left side	852	16	836	46.0	38,456	
Nose	348	8	340	−32.0	−10,880	
Total			2,006		65,756	32.8

Figure 3-5. *Locating the CG of an airplane relative to the datum.*

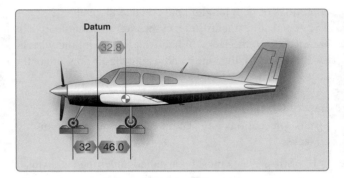

Figure 3-6. *The datum is located at the firewall.*

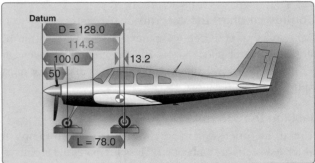

Figure 3-8. *The datum is 100 inches forward of the wing root leading edge.*

off, place chocks around the wheels to keep the airplane from rolling. Subtract the weight of the chocks, called tare weight, from the scale reading to determine the net weight at each weighing point. Multiply each net weight by its arm to determine its moment, and then determine the total weight and total moment. The CG is determined by dividing the total

of the main-wheel weighing points. This is distance (D). The weight of the nosewheel (F) is 340 pounds, and the distance between main wheels and nosewheel (L) is 78 inches. The total weight of the airplane (W) is 2,006 pounds. Determine

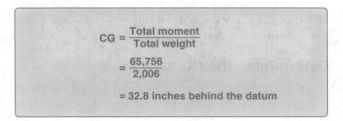

$$CG = \frac{\text{Total moment}}{\text{Total weight}}$$

$$= \frac{65,756}{2,006}$$

$$= 32.8 \text{ inches behind the datum}$$

Figure 3-7. *Determining the CG.*

moment by the total weight. *[Figure 3-7]*
The airplane illustrated in *Figures 3-5* and *3-6* has a net weight of 2,006 pounds, and its CG is 32.8 inches behind the datum.

EWCG Formulas

A chart such as the one in *Figure 3-5* helps the pilot visualize the weights, arms, and moments when solving an EWCG problem, but it is quicker to determine the EWCG by using formulas and an electronic calculator. The use of a calculator for solving these problems is described in Chapter 8, Use of Computers in Weight and Balance Computations.

There are four possible conditions and their formulas that relate the location of CG to the datum. Notice that the formula for each condition first determines the moment of the nosewheel or tailwheel and then divides it by the total weight of the airplane. The arm thus determined is then added to or subtracted from the distance between the main wheels and the datum, distance D.

Datum Forward of the Airplane—Nosewheel Landing Gear

The datum of the airplane in *Figure 3-8* is 100 inches forward of the leading edge of the wing root or 128 inches forward

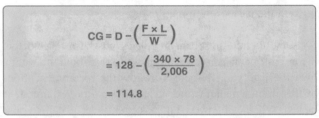

$$CG = D - \left(\frac{F \times L}{W}\right)$$

$$= 128 - \left(\frac{340 \times 78}{2,006}\right)$$

$$= 114.8$$

Figure 3-9. *Determining the CG with datum forward of an airplane with nosewheel landing gear.*

the CG by using the formula in *Figure 3-9*.
The CG is 114.8 inches aft of the datum. This is 13.2 inches forward of the main-wheel weighing points, which proves the location of the datum has no effect on the location of the CG if all measurements are made from the same location.

Datum Aft of the Main Wheels—Nosewheel Landing Gear

The datum of some aircraft may be located aft of the main wheels. The airplane in this example is the same one just discussed, but the datum is at the intersection of the trailing edge of the wing with the fuselage. The distance (D) between the datum of the airplane in *Figure 3-10* and the main-wheel

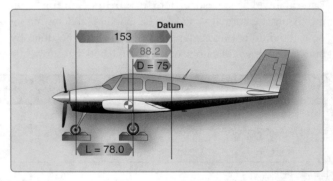

Figure 3-10. *The datum is aft of the main wheels at the wing trailing edge.*

weighing points is 75 inches, the weight of the nosewheel (F) is 340 pounds, and the distance between main wheels and nosewheel (L) is 78 inches. The total net weight of the airplane (W) is 2,006 pounds.

The location of the CG may be determined by using the

$$CG = -\left(D + \frac{F \times L}{W}\right)$$
$$= -\left(75 + \frac{340 \times 78}{2,006}\right)$$
$$= -88.2$$

Figure 3-11. *Determining the CG with datum aft of the main wheels of an airplane with nosewheel landing gear.*

formula in *Figure 3-11*.
The CG location is a negative value, which means it is 88.2 inches forward of the datum. This places it 13.2 inches forward of the main wheels, exactly the same location as when it was measured from other datum locations.

Location of Datum

The location of the datum is not important, but all measurements must be made from the same location.

Datum Forward of the Main Wheels—Tailwheel Landing Gear

Locating the CG of a tailwheel airplane is done in the same way as locating it for a nosewheel airplane except the formula is $\left(\frac{R \times L}{W}\right)$

The distance (D) between the datum of the airplane in *Figure 3-12* and the main-gear weighing points is 7.5 inches, the weight of the tailwheel (R) is 67 pounds, and the distance (L) between the main-wheel and the tailwheel weighing points is 222 inches. The total weight of the airplane (W) is 1,218 pounds. Determine the CG by using the formula in *Figure 3-13*.

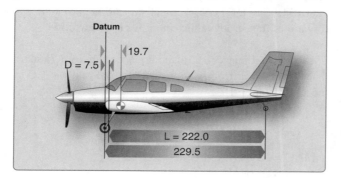

Figure 3-12. *The datum of this tailwheel airplane is the wing root leading edge.*

$$CG = D + \left(\frac{R \times L}{W}\right)$$
$$= 7.5 + \left(\frac{67 \times 222}{1,218}\right)$$
$$= 19.7$$

Figure 3-13. *Determining the CG with datum forward of the main wheels in an airplane with tailwheel landing gear.*

The CG is 19.7 inches behind the datum.
Datum Aft of the Main Wheels—Tailwheel Landing Gear

The datum of the airplane in *Figure 3-14* is located at the intersection of the wing root trailing edge and the fuselage. This places the arm of the main gear (D) at –80 inches. The net weight of the tailwheel (R) is 67 pounds, the distance between the main wheels and the tailwheel (L) is 222 inches, and the total net weight (W) of the airplane is 1,218 pounds. Since the datum is aft of the main wheels, use the formula

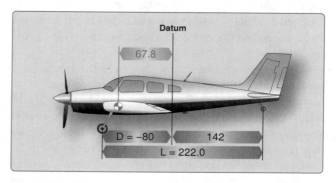

Figure 3-14. *The datum is aft of the main wheels, at the intersection of the wing trailing edge and the fuselage.*

$$CG = -D + \left(\frac{R \times L}{W}\right)$$
$$= -80 + \left(\frac{67 \times 222}{1,218}\right)$$
$$= -67.8$$

Figure 3-16. *Determining the CG with datum aft of the main wheels in an airplane with tailwheel landing gear.*

found in *Figure 3-15*.
The CG is 67.8 inches forward of the datum or 12.2 inches aft of the main-gear weighing points. The CG is in exactly the same location relative to the main wheels, regardless of

where the datum is located.

Center of Gravity (CG) and Mean Aerodynamic Chord (MAC)

Center of Gravity (CG)

In addition to overloading or drastically reducing the aircraft's weight, the distribution of weight is also a concern. When aircraft equipment is changed, the person making the equipment change must make an entry on the equipment list indicating items added, removed, or relocated; the date of the change; and the person's name and certification number in the aircraft's maintenance records.

For the purpose of weight and balance computations, the CG of an airplane is an imaginary point about which the nose-heavy (−) moments and tail-heavy (+) moments are exactly equal in magnitude. If suspended from the CG point, the aircraft would have no tendency to rotate nose up or nose down. The CG of the loaded aircraft can range fore and aft within certain limits that are determined during the flight test for type certification. These limits are the most forward- and rearward-loaded CG positions at which the aircraft meets the performance and flight characteristics required by the FAA.

Any loading that places the CG outside the limits for a particular aircraft seriously impairs the pilot's ability to control the aircraft. For example, it is more difficult to take off and gain altitude in a nose-heavy aircraft, and the aircraft tends to drop its nose when the pilot reduces throttle. It also requires a higher speed to land safely. A tail-heavy aircraft is more susceptible to stalling at low speed, which is a concern during the landing approach.

On small airplanes and on all helicopters, the CG location is identified as being a specific number of inches from the datum. The CG range is identified in the same way. On larger airplanes, from private business jets to large jumbo jets, the CG and its range are typically identified in relation to the width of the wing.

Mean Aerodynamic Chord (MAC)

The width of the wing, or straight-line distance from the leading edge to the trailing edge, on an airplane is known as the chord. If the leading edge and the trailing edge of a wing are parallel, the chord is equal at all points along the entire length of the wing. The average length of the chord, or MAC, of a tapered wing is more complicated to define. The MAC, as seen in *Figure 3-16*, is the chord of an imaginary airfoil that has the same aerodynamic characteristics as the actual airfoil. You can also think of it as the chord drawn through the geographic center of the plan area of the wing.

Usually listed in the aircraft's TCDS when it is required for

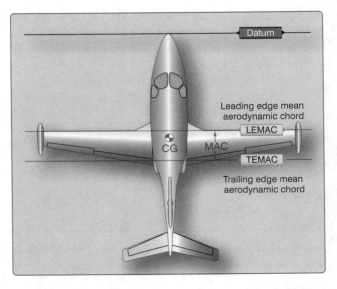

Figure 3-16. *The MAC is the chord drawn through the geographic center of the plan area of the wing.*

weight and balance computations, the MAC is established by the manufacturer, defining its leading edge (LEMAC) and trailing edge (TEMAC) in terms of inches from the datum. *[Figure 3-16]* The CG location and various limits are then expressed in percentage of the chord or percent MAC. In order to relate the percent MAC to the datum, all weight and balance information includes two items: the MAC length in inches and the location of the LEMAC in inches from the datum. For the purpose of simplicity, most light-aircraft manufacturers express the CG range in inches from the datum; transport-category aircraft CGs are expressed in percent MAC.

The relative positions of the CG and the aerodynamic center of lift of the wing have critical effects on the flight characteristics of the aircraft. Consequently, relating the CG location to the chord of the wing is convenient from a design and operations standpoint. Normally, an aircraft has acceptable flight characteristics if the CG is located somewhere near the 25 percent average chord point. This means the CG is located one-fourth of the distance back from the LEMAC to the TEMAC. Such a location places the CG forward of the aerodynamic center for most airfoils.

The weight and balance data of the airplane in *Figure 3-17* states that the MAC is from stations 144 to 206 and the CG is located at station 161.

MAC = TEMAC − LEMAC

MAC = 206" − 144"

MAC = 62"

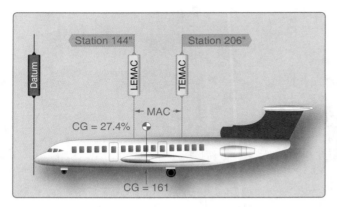

Figure 3-17. *Large aircraft weight and balance calculation diagram.*

CG = 161"

In order to find the percent MAC, first determine the distance of the CG from LEMAC.

CG − LEMAC = Distance from LEMAC

161" − 144" = 17"

The location of the CG expressed in percent MAC is

$$CG\ inches\ \%\ MAC = \frac{Distance\ aft\ of\ LEMAC \times 100}{MAC}$$
$$= \frac{17 \times 100}{62}$$
$$= 27.4$$

Figure 3-18. *Formula for determining the CG expressed in percent MAC.*

determined using the formula found in *Figure 3-18*. The CG of the airplane is located at 27.4 percent MAC.

It is sometimes necessary to determine the location of the CG in inches from the datum when its location in percent MAC is known.

The CG of the airplane is located at 27.4 percent MAC.

MAC = 206 − 144 = 62

LEMAC = station 144

$$CG\ inches\ from\ datum = LEMAC + \frac{MAC \times CG\ \%\ MAC}{100}$$
$$= 144 + \frac{62 \times 27.4}{100}$$
$$= 160.9$$

Figure 3-19. *Formula for determining the CG in inches from the datum.*

Determine the location of the CG in inches from the datum by using the formula found in *Figure 3-19*.

The CG of this airplane is located at station 160.9 inches aft of the datum. It is important for longitudinal stability that the CG be located ahead of the center of lift of a wing. Since the center of lift is expressed as percent MAC, the location of the CG is expressed in the same terms.

Chapter 4

Light Sport Aircraft Weight and Balance Control

Introduction

This chapter discusses the weight and balance procedures for light sport aircraft (LSA) that differ from conventional aircraft, specifically weight-shift control (WSC) aircraft (also called trikes), powered parachutes, and amateur-built LSA. *[Figure 4-1]*

N-number:	N 00001
Serial number:	P123456789
Maximum (gross) weight*:	1,100 lb
(−) Empty weight*:	− 435 lb

Flight Test		
	Date	2010
	Front seat weight	215
	Attachment points	3 and 4

Front Seat Weight Range (lb)	CG/Riser Attachment	
	Main riser	Safety riser
275–375	1	
235–335	1	2
205–305		3
175–275	1	4
145–250	2	5
115–225	4	6
90–200v	5	7

Variable Attachment Points on CG Plates

Figure 4-1. *Examples of light sport aircraft (from top left, clockwise): weight-shift control, powered parachute, glider, airplanes, hot air balloon, and amateur-built LSA.*

LSA Definition of Terms

LSA is a category of simple, very basic, small, light-weight, low-performance aircraft, other than a helicopter or powered-lift, and a classification of aircraft specific to the United States. The Federal Aviation Administration (FAA) defines LSA as an aircraft with a maximum gross takeoff weight of not more than 1,320 pounds (600 kg) for aircraft not intended for operation over water, or 1,430 pounds (650 kg) for aircraft intended for operation over water; a maximum airspeed in level flight of 120 knots (220 kilometers per hour (km/h); 140 miles per hour (mph)); a maximum stall speed of 45 knots (83 km/h; 52 mph); a maximum seating capacity of no more than two persons (including the pilot); fixed undercarriage

and fixed-pitch or ground-adjustable propeller; and a single reciprocating engine (if powered).

An aircraft that qualifies as LSA may be operated by the holder of a sport pilot certificate, whether registered as LSA or not. Pilots with a private, recreational, or higher pilot certificate may also fly LSA, even if their medical certificates have expired, as long as they have a valid driver's license to prove that they are in good enough health to fly. LSA also have less restrictive maintenance requirements and may be maintained and inspected by traditionally certificated aircraft maintenance technicians (AMTs) or by individuals holding a Repairman: Light Sport certificate, and (in some cases) by their pilots and/or owners.

Weight and Balance

Aircraft such as balloons, powered parachutes, and WSC do not require weight and balance computations because the load is suspended below the lifting mechanism. The CG range in these types of aircraft is such that it is difficult to exceed CG limits. For example, the rear seat position and fuel of a WSC aircraft are as close as possible to the hang point with the aircraft in a suspended attitude. Thus, load variations have little effect on the CG. This also holds true for lighter-than-air aircraft, such as a balloon basket or gondola. While it is difficult to exceed CG limits in these aircraft, pilots should never overload an aircraft, as doing so may cause structural damage and/or failures.

Weight affects performance; therefore, pilots should calculate weight and remain within the manufacturer's established limits at all times.

WSC Aircraft

WSC aircraft are one- and two-place aircraft that exceed the criteria of an ultra-light vehicle but do meet the criteria of an LSA. The definition for WSC can be found in 14 CFR part 1. A WSC aircraft used for sport and private pilot flying must be registered with an FAA N-number, have an airworthiness certificate, a pilot's operating handbook (POH), and/or limitations with a weight and loading document aboard.

As mentioned earlier, WSC aircraft are commonly called trikes. These aircraft have few options for loading because they lack places to put useful load items. One-place trikes have only one seat and a fuel tank, which means the only variables for a flight are amount of fuel and weight of the pilot. Two-place trikes can accommodate a pilot and a passenger. This version may have a small storage bin in addition to the fuel tank.

The most significant factor affecting the weight and balance of a trike is the weight of the pilot and, if the aircraft has two seats, the weight of the passenger. The trike acts somewhat like a single, main-rotor helicopter because the weight of the aircraft hangs like a pendulum under the wing. *Figure 4-2* shows a two-place trike, in which the mast and the nose strut come together slightly below the wing attach point. When the trike is in flight, the weight of the aircraft hangs from the wing attach point. The weight of the engine and fuel is behind this point, the passenger is almost directly below this point, and the pilot is forward of this point. The balance of the aircraft is determined by how all these weights compare. The wing attach point, with respect to the wing keel, is an adjustable location. The attach point is moved slightly forward or slightly aft, depending on the weight of the occupants. For

- CG is under wing hang point for level flight.
- Center of lift is directly above CG, above the wing hang point for level flight.

Thrust line is typically designed to be at vertical CG.

Aircraft CG

Fuel tank

CG

Figure 4-2. *CG of a trike.*

example, if the aircraft is flown by a heavy person, the attach point can be moved farther aft, bringing the wing forward to compensate for the change in CG. *Figure 4-3* shows a close-up of the wing attach point and the small amount of forward and aft movement that is available.

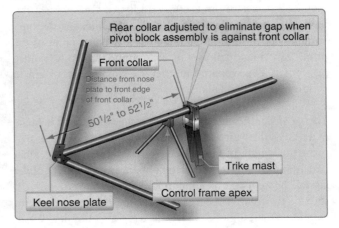

Figure 4-3. *Wing attach point.*

Similar to airplanes, sailplanes, and powered parachutes, increasing weight creates increases in speed and descent rate. However, the WSC aircraft has a unique characteristic. Adding weight to a WSC aircraft creates more twist in the wing because the outboard leading edges flex more. With less lift at the tips, a nose-up effect is created and the trim speed lowers. Therefore, adding weight can increase speed similar to other aircraft, but reduce the trim speed because of the increased twist unique to the WSC aircraft. Each manufacturer's make/model has different effects depending on the specific design. For detailed weight and balance information, characteristics, and operating limitations, always reference the specific manufacturer's manual or POH for the make and model. *Figure 4-4* shows an example of a weight and loading sheet that would be issued with a WSC aircraft. Every aircraft has its own weight and loading data that should come from the manufacturer. The example in *Figure 4-4* comes from Airborne, an Australian company, named Airborne XT WSC aircraft. For additional information, refer to the Weight-Shift Control Aircraft Flying Handbook (FAA-H-8083-5).

Powered Parachutes

Powered parachutes have many of the same characteristics as WSC aircraft when it comes to weight and balance. They have the same limited loading, with only one or two seats, and a fuel tank. A powered parachute acts like a pendulum with the weight of the aircraft hanging beneath the inflated wing (parachute). The point at which the inflated wing attaches to the structure of the aircraft is adjustable to compensate for pilots and passengers of varying weights. With a very heavy pilot, the wing attach point would be moved forward to prevent the aircraft from being too nose heavy. *Figure 4-5* illustrates the structure of a powered parachute and the location of the wing attachment.

A powered parachute used for sport and private flying must be registered with an FAA N-number, have an airworthiness certificate, a POH, and/or limitations with a weight and balance document aboard. The aircraft must be maintained properly by the aircraft owner, or other qualified personnel, and have the aircraft logbooks available for inspection. Always refer to the POH for weight and balance information specific to the powered parachute being flown. For additional information, refer to the Powered Parachute Flying Handbook (FAA-H-8083-29).

Weight and Balance Computations (Amateur-Built Aircraft)

A good weight and balance calculation is the keystone of flight testing an amateur-built aircraft. Accurately determining the aircraft's takeoff weight and ensuring that the CG is within the aircraft's design for each flight is critical to conducting a safe flight test.

The aircraft should be level when weighed, spanwise and fore and aft in accordance with the kit manufacturer's instructions, and should be in the level flight position. It is highly recommended that the aircraft be weighed in an enclosed area using three calibrated scales. Bathroom scales are not recommended because they are not always accurate.

Make and (trike) base model **Airborne XT series/X series aircraft**
Applicable wing models **Airborne streak 3/Streak 2B/Cruze/Wizard wing**

Date		Registration	
Empty weight		Wing model	
Maximum takeoff weight		Serial number	

The effect of changing the hang position is to change the trim speed of the aircraft. Moving the hang point forward increases trim speed (shorter distances to the datum). The hang point position range may be used on the applicable wings for the entire weight range of the aircraft. CG limits on the trike base/gondola section of the aircraft limits are not critical. The defined hang point position and its limits are defined in this document.

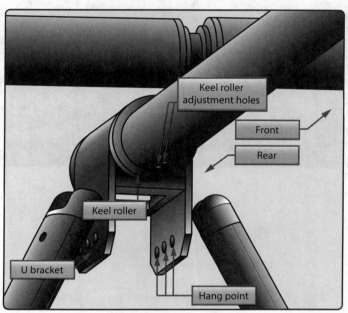

The datum point is the forward bolt on the nose plate (a line between the leading edge pivot bolts on the nose plate) referenced to the hang bolt at the top of the mast for the trike base (gondola).

Moving hang point position is made by moving the keel roller forward or backward along the keel or by moving the hang point within the U-bracket. A sticker is used on the keel to show the standard position for the keel roller. It lists the keel tube holes used as standard trim points for each model wing. The table below shows the standard keel roller position and the allowable range of CG position/hang bolt position referenced to the nose plate datum.

Diagram of the wing hang point construction, showing keel, U-bracket, and the top of the control frame.

Wing model and maximum takeoff weight	Standard trim position and range Distance from the forward keel roller bolt to forward nose plate bolt	Distance from the hang point to forward nose-plate bolt Permissible rear and foremost positions Permissible U-bracket holes
Streak 3 MTO@ 450 kg	Keel hole 2, second from front **1,340 mm +0 – 20 mm**	**1,293.5 mm (54.9 in)** rear limit **1,353.5 mm (53.3 in)** forward limit Middle U-bracket hole only
Streak 2B MTOW 450 kg	Keel hole 3, third from front **1,360 mm ±20 mm**	**1,413.5 mm (55.6 in)** rear limit **1,373.5 mm (54.1 in)** forward limit Front and middle U-bracket hole only
Cruze MTOW 450 kg	Keel hole 3, third from front **1,360 mm ±20 mm**	**1,413.5 mm (55.6 in)** rear limit **1,373.5 mm (54.1 in)** forward limit Middle U-bracket hole only
Wizard MTOW 430 kg	Keel hole 1, at front **1,545 mm +0 – 45 mm**	**1,578.5 mm (61.2 in)** rear limit **1,648.5 mm (64.9 in)** forward limit All U-bracket holes permitted

Figure 4-4. *Weight and loading for WSC aircraft.*

Figure 4-8. *Powered parachute.*

Chapter 5

Single-Engine Aircraft Weight and Balance Computations

Introduction

Weight and balance data allows the pilot to determine the loaded weight of the aircraft and determine whether or not the loaded center of gravity (CG) is within the allowable range for the weight. See *Figure 5-1* for an example of the data necessary for these calculations.

Airplane basic empty weight	1,874.0 lb, EWCG +36.1
CG range	(+40.9) to (+46.0) at 3,100 lb
	(+33.0) to (+46.0) at 2,250 lb or less
	Straight line variation between points given
Empty weight CG range	None
Maximum weight	3,100 lb takeoff/flight
	2,950 lb landing
No. of seats	4 (2 front at +37.0)
	(2 rear at +74.0)
Maximum baggage	160 lb
	Area A (100 lb at +97.0)
	Area B (60 lb at +116.0)
Fuel capacity	92 gal (88 gal usable); two 46 gal integral tanks in wings at +46.6
Oil capacity	12 qt (−15)

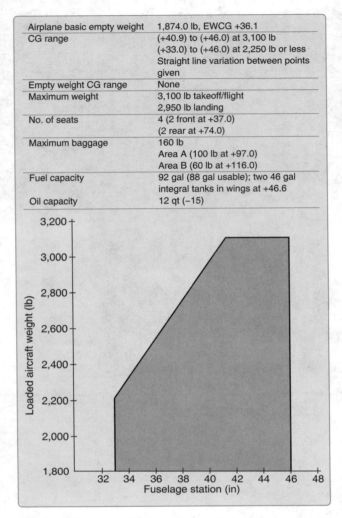

Figure 5-1. *Weight and balance data needed to determine proper loading of a small airplane.*

Determining the Loaded Weight and CG

An important part of preflight planning is determining that the aircraft is loaded so its weight and CG location are within the allowable limits. The methods of accomplishing this are the manual computational method using weights, arms, and moments; the chart method using weight and moment indexes *[Figure 5-2];* and the loading graph method, which eliminates the need for some mathematical calculations.

Manual Computational Method

The manual computational method uses weights, arms, and moments. It relates the total weight and CG location to a CG limits chart similar to those included in the Type Certificate Data Sheet (TCDS) and the Pilot's Operating Handbook/ Aircraft Flight Manual (POH/AFM).

A worksheet, such as the one shown in *Figure 5-3,* provides a means to record and compute pertinent weights, arms, and

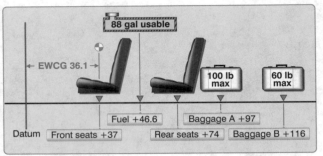

Figure 5-2. *Airplane loading diagram.*

moments for all onboard fuel, personnel, equipment, cargo, and baggage that is not included in the aircraft's basic empty weight (BEW). *Figure 5-4* is a sample of a typical equipment list where many of the pertinent weights and moment values can be found.

As part of preflight planning, fill in the blanks in the worksheet with the specific data for the flight. The following weights were used to complete the sample weight and balance worksheet in *Figure 5-3.*

Pilot	120 lb
Front seat passenger	180 lb
Rear seat passenger	175 lb
Fuel (88 gal)	528 lb
Baggage A	100 lb
Baggage B	50 lb

Multiply each item's weight by its arm to determine the moment. Then, determine the total weight and the sum of the moments. Divide the total moment by the total weight to determine the CG in inches from the datum. For this example, the total weight is 3,027 pounds and the CG is 43.54 inches aft of the datum (a negative result would have indicated a CG forward of the datum).

To determine whether or not the airplane is properly loaded for this flight, use the CG limits chart. *[Figure 5-5]* Draw a line vertically upward from the CG of 43.54 inches and one horizontally to the right from the loaded weight of 3,027 pounds. These lines cross inside the envelope, which shows the airplane is properly loaded for takeoff, but 77 pounds overweight for landing. Note that for this sample chart, the envelope is defined by the solid black line that indicates CG limits at or below the maximum weight for takeoff and landing. There is an additional region identified by a segmented black line that includes weights suitable only for takeoff. It is important to note these subtle differences as they may or may not be found in every POH/AFM.

Item	Weight (3,100 lb max.) [X]	Arm (in) [=]	Moment (lb-in)	CG (inches from datum)
Airplane	1,874	36.1	67,651.4	
Front seats	300	37.0	11,100.0	
Rear seats	175	74.0	12,950.0	
Fuel (88 gal usable)	528	46.6	24,604.8	
Baggage A (100 max.)	100	97.0	9,700.0	
Baggage B (60 max.)	50	116.0	5,800.0	
	3,027		131,806.2	+43.54

Figure 5-3. *Loading schedule chart derived from loading problem.*

Item Number	Equipment List Description	Ref Drawing	Wt (lb)	Arm (in)
24-04-S	Basic Avionics Kit Installation		4.3*	55.5*
	- Support Straps Installation		0.1	10.0
	- Avionics Cooling Fan Installation		1.6	3.0
	- Avionics Ground Installations		0.1	41.0
	- Circuit Breaker Panel Installation		1.5	16.5
	- Microphone Installation		0.2	18.5
	- Omni Antenna Installation		0.5	252.1
	- Omni Antenna Cable Assembly Installation		0.3	248.0
	Chapter 25—Equipment/Furnishings			
25-01-R	Seat, Pilot, Adjustable		33.8	41.5
25-02-S	Seat, Copilot, Adjustable		33.8	41.5
25-03-S	Seat, Rear, Two Piece Back Cushion		50.0	82.0
25-04-R	Seat Belt and Shoulder Harness, Inertia Reel, Pilot and Copilot		5.2	50.3
25-05-S	Seat Belt and Shoulder Harness, Inertia Reel, Rear Seat		5.2	87.8
25-06-S	Sun Visors (Set of 2)		1.2	33.0
25-07-S	Baggage Retaining Net		0.5	108.0
25-08-S	Cargo Tie Down Rings (10 Tie Downs)		0.4	108.0
25-09-S	Pilot's Operating Checklist (Stowed in Instrument Panel Map Case)		0.3	15.0
25-10-R	Pilot's Operating Handbook and FAA-Approved Airplane Flight Manual (Stowed in Pilot's Seat Back)		1.2	61.5
25-11-S	Fuel Sampling Cup		0.1	14.3
25-12-S	Tow Bar, Nose Gear (Stowed)		1.7	108.0
25-13-S	Emergency Locator Transmitter Installation		2.2*	134.8*
	- ELT Transmitter		1.7	135.0
	- Antenna and Cable Assembly		0.4	133.0
	- Hardware		0.1	138.0
	Chapter 26—Fire Protection			
26-01-S	Fire Extinguisher Installation		5.3*	29.0*
	- Fire Extinguisher		4.8	29.0
	- Mounting Clamp and Hardware		0.5	29.0
	Chapter 27—Flight Controls			
27-01-S	Dual Controls Installation, Right Seat		6.3*	12.9*
	- Control Wheel, Copilot		2.0	26.0
	- Rudder and Brake Pedal Installation Copilot		4.3	6.8

* Indicates total weight/arm for all subcomponents

Figure 5-4. *Typical equipment list.*

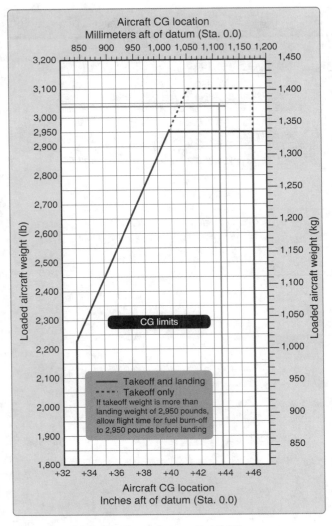

Figure 5-5. *CG limits chart from a typical POH.*

Loading Graph Method

The charts and graphs found in the POH/AFM can help simplify and expedite the preflight weight and balance computation process. Some use a loading graph and moment indexes rather than the arms and moments. These charts eliminate the need for calculating moments and make computations quicker and easier. *[Figure 5-6]*

Moment Indexes

Moments determined by multiplying the weight of each component by its arm result in large numbers that are awkward to calculate and can become a source of mathematical error. To eliminate these large numbers, moment indexes are sometimes used. The moment is divided by a reduction factor, such as 100 or 1,000, to get the moment index. The loading graph provides the moment index for each component to avoid mathematical calculations. The CG envelope uses moment indexes rather than arms and moments.

The CG limits envelope is the enclosed area on a graph of the airplane loaded weight and the CG location. If lines drawn from the weight and CG cross within this envelope, the airplane is properly loaded.

Loading Graph

Figure 5-6 is a typical loading graph taken from the POH of a modern four-place airplane. It is a graph of load weight and load moment indexes. Diagonal lines for each item relate the weight to the moment index without having to use mathematical calculations.

Compute Weight and Balance Using the Loading Graph

To compute the weight and balance using the loading graph in *Figure 5-6*, make a loading schedule chart like the one in *Figure 5-7*. In *Figure 5-6*, follow the horizontal line for 300 pounds load weight to the right until it intersects the diagonal line for pilot and front passenger. From this point, drop a line vertically to the load moment index along the bottom to determine the load moment for the front seat occupants. This is 11.1 lb-in divided by 1,000. Record it in the loading schedule chart. Determine the load moment for the 175 pounds of rear seat occupants along the diagonal for second row passengers or cargo. This is 12.9; record it in the loading schedule chart.

Determine the load moment for the fuel and the baggage in areas A and B in the same way and enter them all in the loading schedule chart. The maximum fuel is marked on the diagonal line for fuel in terms of gallons or liters. The maximum is 88 gallons of usable fuel. The total capacity is 92 gallons, but in our example, 4 gallons are unusable and have already been included in the empty weight of the aircraft. The weight of 88 gallons of fuel is 528 pounds and its moment index is 24.6. The 100 pounds of baggage in area A has a moment index of 9.7 and the 50 pounds in area B has an index of 5.8. Enter all of these weights and moment indexes in the loading schedule chart and add all of the weights and moment indexes to determine the totals.

Transfer totals to the CG moment envelope in *Figure 5-8*. The CG moment envelope is an enclosed area on a graph of the airplane loaded weight and loaded moment. If lines drawn from the weight and loaded moment cross within this envelope, the airplane is properly loaded. The loading schedule from the example in *Figure 5-7* shows that the total weight of the loaded aircraft is 3,027 pounds, and the loaded airplane moment divided by 1,000 is 131.8.

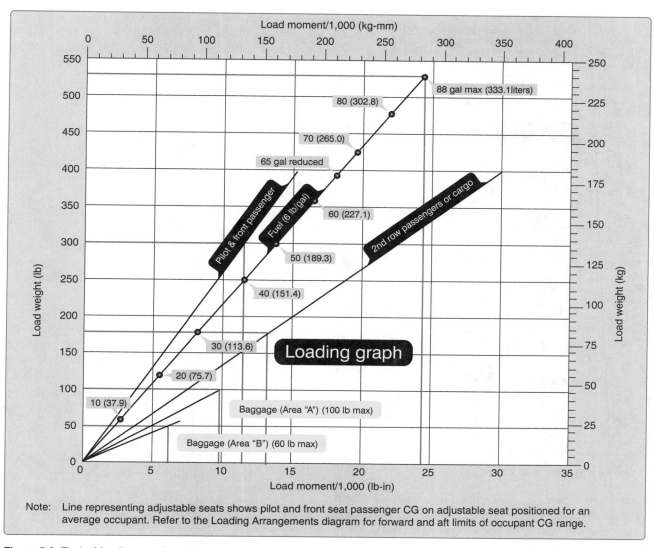

Figure 5-6. *Typical loading graph.*

Item	Weight	Moment/1,000
Airplane (BEW)	1,874	67.7
Front seats	300	11.1
Rear seats	175	12.9
Fuel	528	24.6
Baggage A	100	9.7
Baggage B	50	5.8
Total	3,027	131.8

Figure 5-7. *Loading schedule chart.*

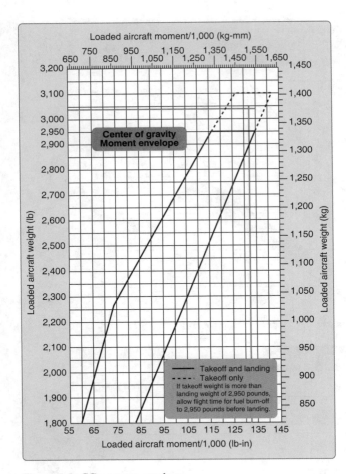

Figure 5-8. *CG moment envelope.*

Referring to *Figure 5-8*, draw a line vertically upward from 131.8 on the horizontal index at the bottom of the chart and a horizontal line from 3,027 pounds in the left-vertical index. These lines intersect within the dashed area, which shows that the aircraft is loaded properly for takeoff, but it is too heavy for landing (similar to the previous example). Because of this, if the aircraft had to return for landing immediately after takeoff, it would need to fly long enough to burn 77 pounds (slightly less than 13 gallons) of fuel to reduce its weight for landing.

Chapter 6
Multiengine Aircraft Weight and Balance Computations

Introduction

Weight and balance computations for small multiengine airplanes are similar to those discussed for single-engine airplanes. See *Figure 6-1* for an example of weight and balance data for a typical light twin-engine airplane.

Item	Weight (lbs) (5,200 max.)	Arm (in)	Moment (lb-in)	CG
Engines	3,494	35.28	120,093	
Fuel (144 gal)	840	61.0	51,240	
Front seat	320	37.0	11,840	
Row 2 seats	310	75.0	23,250	
Fwd baggage	100	-15.0	-1,500	
Aft baggage	90	113.0	10,170	
Total	5,004		215,093	42.47

eight	Front seats Arm +_	Row 2 seats Arm +142
100	1_	142
110		156
120		170
130		185
140		199
150		213
160		227
		241
		256

Datum	Forward face of fuselage bulkhead ahead of rudder pedals
Seats	2 at 37.0 2 at 75.0 1 at 113.0: 200 lb limit
Fuel	213.4 gal (2 wing tanks, 105.0 gal each 103.0 gal usable at +61.0) Undrainable fuel: 1.6 lb at +62
Oil	24 quarts (12 quarts in each engine): −3.3
Baggage	Forward 100 lb limit : −15 Aft 200 lb limit: +113
CG Range	(+38) to (+43.1) at 5,200 lb (+43.6) at 4,800 lb (+32) to (+43.6) at 4,300 lb or less Straight line variation between points given
Engine	2 240-horsepower horizontally opposed engines Fuel burn: 24 gph for 65% cruise at 175 knots 29 gph for 75% cruise at 180 knots

Figure 6-1. *Typical weight and balance data for a light twin-engine airplane.*

The airplane in this example was weighed to determine its basic empty weight (BEW) and empty weight center of gravity (EWCG). The weighing conditions and results are:

Weight with fuel drained and oil full:

Right wheel scales........................1,084 lb, tare 8 lb

Left wheel scales ....1,148 lb, tare 8 lb

Nose wheel scales.......................1,202 lb, tare 14 lb

Determine the Loaded CG

First, add the weights indicated by the individual scales and then subtract the tare weights to determine the BEW. Next, using the BEW and EWCG, the loaded weight and CG of the aircraft can be determined with data from *Figure 6-2*, using a chart such as the one in *Figure 6-3*.

The aircraft is loaded as shown:

Fuel (140 gal) .... 840 lb

Front seats .... 320 lb

Row 2 seats.. 310 lb

Forward baggage .... 100 lb

Aft baggage .... 90 lb

Chart Method Using Weight, Arm, and Moments

Make a chart showing the weight, arm, and moments of the airplane and its load.

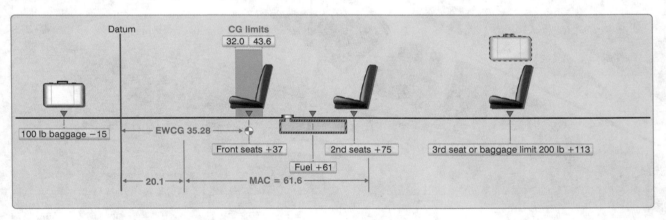

Figure 6-2. *Twin-engine airplane weight and balance diagram.*

Item	Weight (lb) (5,200 max.) [X]	Arm (in) [=]	Moment (lb-in)	CG
Airplane	3,404	35.28	120,093	
Fuel (140 gal)	840	61.0	51,240	
Front seat	320	37.0	11,840	
Row 2 seats	310	75.0	23,250	
Foward baggage	100	−15.0	−1,500	
Aft baggage	90	113.0	10,170	
Total	5,064		215,093	42.47

Figure 6-3. *Determining the loaded CG of the sample airplane in Figure 6-2.*

The loaded weight for this flight is 5,064 pounds, and the CG is located at 42.47 inches aft of the datum.

To determine that the weight and CG are within the allowable range, refer to the CG range chart in *Figure 6-4*. Draw a line vertically upward from 42.47 inches from the datum and one horizontally from 5,064 pounds. These lines cross inside the envelope, showing that the airplane is properly loaded.

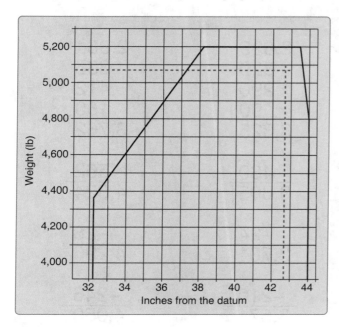

Figure 6-4. *Sample CG range chart.*

Determining the CG in Percentage of Mean Aerodynamic Chord (MAC)

Refer again to *Figures 6-2* and *6-3*.

The loaded CG is 42.47 inches aft of the datum.

The MAC is 61.6 inches long.

The LEMAC is located at station 20.1.

The CG is 42.47 – 20.1 = 22.37 inches aft of LEMAC.

Use the formula in *Figure 6-5* to find the CG in percent MAC.

$$CG\ in\ \%\ MAC = \frac{CG\ in\ inches\ from\ LEMAC \times 100}{MAC}$$

$$= \frac{22.37 \times 100}{61.6}$$

$$= 36.3\%\ MAC$$

Figure 6-5. *Finding CG in percent MAC.*

The loaded CG is located at 36.3 percent MAC.

The Chart Method Using Weight and Moment Indexes

As mentioned in the previous chapter, anything that can be done to make careful preflight planning easier makes flying safer. Many manufacturers furnish charts in the Pilot's Operating Handbook/Aircraft Flight Manual (POH/AFM) that use weight and moment indexes rather than weight, arm, and moments. The charts also help reduce errors by including tables of moment indexes for the various weights.

Consider the loading for this particular flight:

　　Cruise fuel flow = 16 gallons per hour

　　Estimated time en route = 2 hours, 10 minutes

　　Reserve fuel = 45 minutes = 12 gallons

　　Total required fuel = 47 gallons

The pilot completes a chart like the one in *Figure 6-6* using moment indexes from tables in *Figures 6-7* and *6-8*.

The moments divided by 100 in the index column are found in the charts in *Figures 6-7* through *6-9*. If the exact weight is not in the chart, interpolate between the weights that are included. When a weight is greater than any of those shown in the charts, add the moment indexes for a combination of weights to get that which is desired. For example, to get the moments divided by 100 for the 320 pounds in the front seats, add the moment index for 100 pounds (105) to that for 220 pounds (231). This gives the moment index of 336 for 320 pounds in the front seats.

Use the moment limits versus weight envelope in *Figure 6-10* to determine if the weight and balance conditions are within allowable limits for both takeoff and landing at the destination. The moment limits versus weight envelope is an enclosed area on a graph of three parameters. The diagonal line representing the moment divided by 100 crosses the horizontal line representing the weight at the vertical line representing the CG location in inches aft of the datum. When the lines cross inside the envelope, the aircraft is loaded within its weight and CG limits.

　　Takeoff: – 3,781 lb and 4,296 moment divided by 100

　　Landing: – 3,571 lb and 4,050 moment divided by 100

Weight and Balance Loading Form

Model _____   Date _____

Serial Number _____   Reg. Number _____

Item	Pounds (3,900 max.)	Index moment/100
Airplane basic empty weight	2,625	2,864
Front seat occupants	320	336
Row 2 seats	290	412
Baggage (200 lb max.)	90	150
Subtotal	3,325	3,762
Zero fuel condition (3,500 max.)		
Fuel loading (gallons) 80	480	562
Subtotal	3,805	4,324
Ramp condition		
* Less fuel for start, taxi, and takeoff	−24	−28
Subtotal	3,781	4,296
Takeoff condition		
Less fuel to destination (gallons) 35	−210	−246
Landing condition	3,571	4,050

* Fuel for start, taxi, and takeoff is normally 24 pounds at a moment index of 28.

Figure 6-6. *Typical weight and balance loading form.*

Occupant Moments/100		
Weight	Front seats Arm +105	Row 2 seats Arm +142
100	105	142
110	116	156
120	126	170
130	137	185
140	147	199
150	158	213
160	168	227
170	179	241
180	189	256
190	200	270
200	210	284
210	221	298
220	231	312
230	242	327
240	252	341
250	263	355

Figure 6-7. *Sample weight and moment index for occupants.*

Locate the moment divided by 100 diagonal line for 4,296 and follow it down until it crosses the horizontal line for 3,781 pounds. These lines cross inside the envelope at the vertical line for a CG location of 114 (113.6) inches aft of the datum.

The maximum allowable takeoff weight is 3,900 pounds, and this airplane weighs 3,781 pounds. The CG limits for 3,781 pounds are 109.8 to 117.5. The CG of 114 (113.6) inches falls within these allowable limits.

Baggage Moments/100	
Weight	Arm +167
10	17
20	33
30	50
40	67
50	84
60	100
70	117
80	134
90	150
100	167
110	184
120	200
130	217
140	234
150	251
160	267
170	284
180	301
190	317
200	334

Figure 6-8. *Sample weight and moment index for baggage.*

Usable Fuel – Arm +117		
Gallons	Pounds	Moment/100
10	60	70
20	120	140
30	180	211
40	240	281
50	300	351
60	360	421
70	420	491
80	480	562
90	540	632
100	600	702

Figure 6-9. *Sample weight and moment index for fuel.*

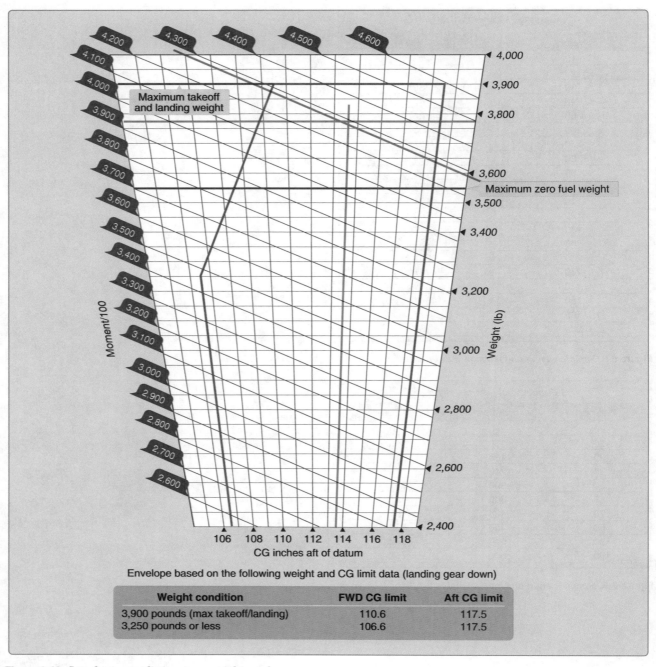

Figure 6-10. *Sample moment limits versus weight envelope.*

Chapter 7

Center of Gravity Change After a Repair or Alteration

Introduction

The largest weight changes that occur during the lifetime of an aircraft are those caused by alterations and repairs. It is the responsibility of the FAA-certificated mechanic or repairman doing the work to accurately document the weight change and record it in both the maintenance records and the Pilot's Operating Handbook/Aircraft Flight Manual (POH/AFM).

Weight & Balance
Cessna 182L
N42565
S/N 18259080

Removed the following equipment:

1. Turn coordinator P/N C661003-0201
2. Directional gyro P/N 0706000

Total

1,876
−5

Aircraft after removal: 1,870

Installed the following equipment:

Weigh
13 l

1. S-TEC System 40 autopilot, includes turn coordinator and directional gyro

1,870.38
+13.00
1,883.38

*REVISED LICENSED EMPTY WEIGHT NEW USEFUL LOAD 1,216.62

Forward check (Limit +33.0)

Rear

	Wt.	Arm	Moment
A/C empty	1,883.38	36.18	68,144.15
Fwd. seats	170.00	37.00	6,290.00
Aft seats			

A/C empty
Fwd. seats
Aft seats

$$CG \text{ in } \% \text{ MAC} = \frac{CG \text{ in inches from LEMAC} \times 100}{MAC}$$

$$= \frac{10.42 \times 100}{58.0}$$

$$= 17.9\% \text{ MAC}$$

Weight and Balance Record
(Continuous history of changes in structure or equipment affecting weight and balance)

Airplane Model   Cessna 182L

Serial Number   18259080

Page Numbe

Date	Item No. In	Item No. Out	Description of Article or Modification	Added (+) Wt. (lb)	Added (+) Arm (in)	Added (+) Moment/ 1,000	Removed (−) Wt. (lb)	Removed (−) Arm (in)	Removed (−) Moment/ 1,000	Basi Wt. (lb)	M
8-7-09			Alteration per FAA Form 337 Dated 8-7-09								
			As delivered							1,876	67
	34-XX		Turn coordinator	7.38							
22-XX	34-XX		Directional gyro			.346					
			Autopilot system				−2.5	15.0	−.037	1,883.4	68.1
				13.0	32.7	.425	−3.12	13.5	−.042	1,880.9	68.1
										1,877.8	68.1
										1,890.8	68.5

Item	Weight (lb)	X	Arm (in)	=	Moment (lb-in)	Most Aft CG +46.0
Airplane (empty)	1,876.0		36.14		67,798.6	
Pilot	170.0		34.0		5,780.0	
Fuel (full tanks − 88 gal)	528.0		48.2		25,449.6	
Rear seat occupants (2)	340.0		74.0		25,160.0	
Baggage A	100.0		97.0		9,700.0	
Baggage B	60.0		116.0		6,960.0	
Total	3,074.0				140,8__.0	+__.0

Equipment List

The Federal Aviation Administration (FAA) considers the addition or removal of equipment included in the Comprehensive Equipment List to be a minor alteration. The weights and arms are included with the items in the equipment list, and these minor alterations can be done and the aircraft approved for return to service by an FAA-certificated mechanic or repairman. The only documentation required is an entry in the aircraft maintenance records and the appropriate change to the weight and balance record in the POH/AFM. [Figure 7-1]

Figure 7-2 is a comprehensive list of all Cessna equipment that is available for the Model 182S airplane. It should not be confused with the airplane-specific equipment list. An airplane-specific list is provided with each individual airplane at delivery and is typically found at the end of the Pilot's Operating Handbook. The following comprehensive equipment list and the airplane-specific list have a similar order of listing.

The comprehensive equipment list provides the following information in column form:

In the Item No column, each item is assigned a coded number. The first two digits of the code represent the assignment of an equipment item within the ATA Specification 100 breakdown (Chapter 11 for Placards, Chapter 21 for Air Conditioning, Chapter 77 for Engine Indicating, etc.). These assignments also correspond to the Maintenance Manual chapter breakdown for the airplane. Items receive a unique sequence number (01, 02, 03, etc.). After the sequence number (and hyphen), a suffix letter is assigned to identify an equipment item as required, standard, or optional. Suffix letters are as follows:

–R = required item or equipment for FAA certification

–S = standard equipment item

–O = optional equipment item replacing required or standard item(s)

–A = optional equipment item that is in addition to required or standard items

In the Equipment List Description column, each item is assigned a descriptive name to help identify its function.

In the Ref Drawing column, a drawing number is provided that corresponds to the item.

Note: Additional equipment must be installed in accordance with the reference drawing, service bulletin, or a separate FAA approval.

In the Wt and Arm columns, you find the weight in pounds and arm in inches of the equipment item.

Notes: Unless otherwise indicated, true values (not net change values) for the weight and arm are shown. Positive arms are distances aft of the airplane datum; negative arms are distances forward of the datum. Asterisks (*) in the weight and arm column indicate complete assembly installations. Some major components of the assembly are listed on the lines immediately following. The sum of these major components does not necessarily equal the complete assembly installation.

Weight and Balance Record
(Continuous history of changes in structure or equipment affecting weight and balance)

Date	Item No. In	Item No. Out	Description of Article or Modification	Weight Change Added (+) Wt. (lb)	Arm (in)	Moment/ 1,000	Weight Change Removed (−) Wt. (lb)	Arm (in)	Moment/ 1,000	Running Basic Empty Weight Wt. (lb)	Moment/ 1,000
			As delivered							1,876	67.8
8-7-09	Alteration per FAA Form 337										
	Dated 8-7-09			7.38		.346				1,883.4	68.1
		34-XX	Turn coordinator				−2.5	15.0	−.037	1,880.9	68.1
		34-XX	Directional gyro				−3.12	13.5	−.042	1,877.8	68.1
	22-XX		Autopilot system	13.0	32.7	.425				1,890.8	68.5

Airplane Model Cessna 182L   **Serial Number** 18259080   **Page Number** 1

Figure 7-1. *A typical 14 CFR part 23 weight and balance record.*

Item Number	Equipment List Description	Ref Drawing	Wt (lb)	Arm (in)
24-04-S	Basic Avionics Kit Installation		4.3*	55.5*
	- Support Straps Installation		0.1	10.0
	- Avionics Cooling Fan Installation		1.6	3.0
	- Avionics Ground Installations		0.1	41.0
	- Circuit Breaker Panel Installation		1.5	16.5
	- Microphone Installation		0.2	18.5
	- Omni Antenna Installation		0.5	252.1
	- Omni Antenna Cable Assembly Installation		0.3	248.0
	Chapter 25—Equipment/Furnishings			
25-01-R	Seat, Pilot, Adjustable		33.8	41.5
25-02-S	Seat, Copilot, Adjustable		33.8	41.5
25-03-S	Seat, Rear, Two Piece Back Cushion		50.0	82.0
25-04-R	Seat Belt and Shoulder Harness, Inertia Reel, Pilot and Copilot		5.2	50.3
25-05-S	Seat Belt and Shoulder Harness, Inertia Reel, Rear Seat		5.2	87.8
25-06-S	Sun Visors (Set of 2)		1.2	33.0
25-07-S	Baggage Retaining Net		0.5	108.0
25-08-S	Cargo Tie Down Rings (10 Tie Downs)		0.4	108.0
25-09-S	Pilot's Operating Checklist (Stowed in Instrument Panel Map Case)		0.3	15.0
25-10-R	Pilot's Operating Handbook and FAA-Approved Airplane Flight Manual (Stowed in Pilot's Seat Back)		1.2	61.5
25-11-S	Fuel Sampling Cup		0.1	14.3
25-12-S	Tow Bar, Nose Gear (Stowed)		1.7	108.0
25-13-S	Emergency Locator Transmitter Installation		2.2*	134.8*
	- ELT Transmitter		1.7	135.0
	- Antenna and Cable Assembly		0.4	133.0
	- Hardware		0.1	138.0
	Chapter 26—Fire Protection			
26-01-S	Fire Extinguisher Installation		5.3*	29.0*
	- Fire Extinguisher		4.8	29.0
	- Mounting Clamp and Hardware		0.5	29.0
	Chapter 27—Flight Controls			
27-01-S	Dual Controls Installation, Right Seat		6.3*	12.9*
	- Control Wheel, Copilot		2.0	26.0
	- Rudder and Brake Pedal Installation Copilot		4.3	6.8

* Indicates total weight/arm for all subcomponents

Figure 7-2. *Typical comprehensive equipment list.*

Major Alteration and Repair

Within the following text, information concerning major repairs or major alterations does not apply to any aircraft within the light-sport category. This category of aircraft is not eligible for major repairs or alterations.

Any major alteration or repair requires the work to be done by an FAA-certificated mechanic or repairman or facility. The work must be checked for conformity to FAA-approved data and signed off by an aircraft mechanic holding an Inspection Authorization (IA) or by an authorized agent of an appropriately rated FAA-approved repair station. A Repair Station record and/or FAA form 337, Major Repair and Alteration, must be completed describing the work. (Reference Title 14 of the Code of Federal Regulations (14 CFR) part 43, appendix B, for the recording of major repair and alterations requirements.) A dated and signed revision to the weight and balance record is made and kept with the maintenance records, and the airplane's new empty weight and empty weight arm or moment index are entered in the POH/AFM.

Weight and Balance Revision Record

Aircraft manufacturers use different formats for their weight and balance data, but *Figure 7-3* is typical of a weight and balance revision record. All weight and balance records should be kept with the other aircraft records. Each revision record should be identified by the date, the aircraft make, model, and serial number. The pages should be signed by the person making the revision and his or her certificate type and number must be included.

The computations for a weight and balance revision are included on a weight and balance revision form. Appropriate fore-and-aft extreme loading conditions should be investigated and the computations shown. The date those computations were made is shown in the upper right corner of *Figure 7-3*. When this work is superseded, a notation must be made on the new weight and balance revision form, including a statement that the new computations supersede the computations dated "MM/DD/YY."

Weight & Balance
Cessna 182L
N42565
S/N 18259080

Date: 08/07/09

Supersedes computations of FAA Form 337 dated 10/02/07.

Removed the following equipment:

	Weight	x	Arm	=	Moment
	2.50 lb		15.0		37.50
	+3.12 lb		13.5		+42.12
Total	5.62				79.62

1. Turn coordinator P/N C661003-0201
2. Directional gyro P/N 0706000

	Weight	Arm	Moment
	1,876.00	36.14	67,798.64
	−5.62		−79.62
Aircraft after removal:	1,870.38	36.20	67,719.02

Installed the following equipment:

	Weight	x	Arm	=	Moment
	13 lb		32.70		425.13

1. S-TEC System 40 autopilot, includes turn coordinator and directional gyro

	Weight	Arm	Moment
	1,870.38	36.20	67,719.02
	+13.00		+425.13
	1,883.38	36.18	68,144.15

*REVISED LICENSED EMPTY WEIGHT NEW USEFUL LOAD 1,216.62

Forward check (Limit +33.0)

	Wt.	x	Arm	=	Moment
A/C empty	1,883.38		36.18		68,144.15
Fwd. seats	170.00		37.00		6,290.00
Aft seats					
Fuel (min.)	115.00		48.00		5,520.00
Baggage A					
Baggage B					
	2,168.38		+36.87		79,954.15

Rearward check (Limit +46.0)

	Wt.	x	Arm	=	Moment
A/C empty	1,883.38		36.18		68,144.15
Fwd. seats	170.00		37.00		6,290.00
Aft seats	340.00		74.00		25,160.00
Fuel (min.)	528.00		48.20		25,449.60
Baggage A	100.00		97.00		9,700.00
Baggage B	60.00		116.00		6,960.00
	3,081.38		45.98		141,703.75

Joseph P. Kline

Jeseph P. Kline
A&P 123456789

Figure 7-3. *A typical airplane weight and balance revision record.*

The weight and balance revision sheet should clearly show the revised empty weight, empty weight arm and/or moment index, and the new useful load. An example of these entries can be found at the bottom of *Figure 7-3*.

Weight Changes Caused by a Repair or Alteration

A typical alteration might consist of removing two pieces of radio equipment from the instrument panel and a power supply that was located in the baggage compartment behind the rear seat. In this example, these two pieces are replaced with a single lightweight, self-contained radio. At the same time, an old emergency locator transmitter (ELT) is removed from its mount near the tail, and a lighter weight unit is installed. A passenger seat is installed in the baggage compartment.

Computations Using Weight, Arm, and Moment

The first step in the weight and balance computation is to make a chart like the one in *Figure 7-4*, listing all of the items that are involved. The new center of gravity (CG) of 36.4 inches aft of the datum is determined by dividing the new moment by the new weight.

Computations Using Weight and Moment Indexes

If the weight and balance data uses moment indexes rather than arms and moments, this same alteration can be computed using a chart such as the one in *Figure 7-5*. Subtract the weight and moment indexes of all the removed equipment from the empty weight and moment index of the airplane. Add the weight and moment indexes of all equipment installed to determine the total weight and the total moment index. To determine the position of the new CG in inches aft of the datum, multiply the total moment index by 100 to get the moment, and divide this by the total weight to get the new CG.

Item	Weight (lb)	X	Arm (in)	=	Moment (lb-in)	New CG
Airplane	1,876.0		36.1		67,723.6	
Radio removed	−12.2		15.8		−192.8	
Power supply removed	−9.2		95.0		−874.0	
ELT removed	−3.2		135.0		−432.0	
Radio installed	+8.4		14.6		+122.6	
ELT installed	+1.7		135.0		+229.5	
Passenger seat installed	+21.0		97.0		+2,037.0	
Total	1,882.5				68,613.9	+36.4

Figure 7-4. *Weight, arm, and moment changes caused by typical alteration or repair.*

Item	Weight (lb)	Moment indexes (lb-in/100)	New CG (inches from datum)
Airplane	1,876.0	+677.2	
Radio removed	−12.2	−1.93	
Power supply removed	−9.2	−8.74	
ELT removed	−3.2	−4.32	
Radio installed	+8.4	+1.23	
ELT installed	+1.7	+2.29	
Passenger seat installed	+21.0	+20.37	
Total	1,882.5	+686.1	+36.4

Figure 7-5. *Weight and moment index changes caused by a typical alteration or repair.*

Determining the CG in Percentage of Mean Aerodynamic Chord (Percent MAC)

This procedure is the same as found in Chapter 5, Single-Engine Aircraft Weight and Balance Computations. Refer to the load conditions and CG information found in *Figures 7-5, 7-6,* and *7-7* to compute the CG in percent MAC:

The loaded CG is +36.4 inches aft of the datum.

The MAC is 58.0 inches long.

The leading edge mean aerodynamic chord (LEMAC) is located at station 25.98.

The CG is +36.4 − 25.98 = 10.42 inches aft of LEMAC.

Airplane EW and EWCG	1,876.0 lb at +36.14
Engine METO horsepower	230
CG range	(+40.9) to (+46.0) at 3,100 lb
	(+33.0) to (+46.0) at 2,250 lb or less
	Straight line variation between points given
Empty weight CG range	None
Maximum weight	3,100 lb takeoff/flight
	2,950 lb landing
Datum to LEMAC	25.98
MAC	58.00
No. of seats	4 (2 front at +34.0)
	(2 rear at +74.0)
Fuel capacity	92 gal (88 gal usable)
	two 46-gal integral tanks in wings at +48.2
	See NOTE 1 for data on unusable fuel.
Minimum fuel	(METO HP ÷ 2) 115 lb at +48
Maximum baggage	160 lb
	Area A (100 lb at +97.0)
	Area B (60 lb at +116.0)
Oil capacity	12 qt (−15) (6 qt usable)
	See NOTE 1 for data on undrainable oil.

NOTE 1: The certificated empty weight and corresponding center of gravity location must include unusable fuel of 30 lb (+46) and undrainable oil of 0 lb.

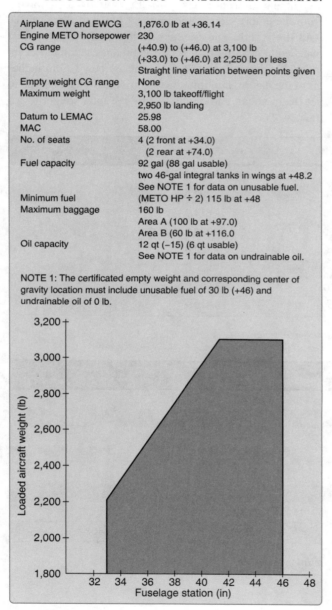

Figure 7-6. *Weight and balance information.*

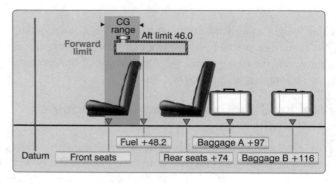

Figure 7-7. *Loading conditions.*

Use the formula in *Figure 7-8* to determine CG in MAC percentages.

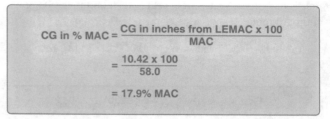

Figure 7-8. *Formula for determining the CG in percent MAC.*

The loaded CG after alteration or repair is located at 17.9 percent MAC.

Empty Weight CG (EWCG) Range

The fuel tanks, seats, and baggage compartments of some aircraft are so located that changes in the fuel or occupant load have a very limited effect on the balance of the aircraft. Aircraft of such a configuration show an empty weight CG (EWCG) range in the Type Certificate Data Sheet (TCDS). If the EWCG is located within this range, it is impossible to legally load the aircraft so that its loaded CG falls outside its allowable range.

If the TCDS lists an EWCG range, and after the alteration is completed the EWCG falls within this range, then there is no need to compute a fore and aft check for adverse loading. But if the TCDS lists the EWCG range as "None" (and most of them do), a check must be made to determine whether or not it is possible by any combination of legal loading to cause the aircraft CG to move outside of either its forward or aft limits.

Adverse-Load CG Checks

Many modern aircraft have multiple rows of seats and often more than one baggage compartment. After any repair or alteration that changes the weight and balance, the Airframe and Powerplant (A&P) FAA-certificated mechanic or repairman must ensure that no legal condition of loading can move the CG outside of its allowable limits. To determine this, adverse-loaded CG checks must be performed and the results noted in the weight and balance revision sheet. [Figure 7-3]

Forward Adverse-Load CG Check

To conduct a forward CG check, make a chart that includes the airplane and any occupants and items of the load located in front of the forward CG limit. Include only those items behind the forward limit that are essential to flight: the pilot, and the minimum fuel.

In this example, the pilot, whose nominal weight is 170 pounds, is behind the forward CG limit. The fuel is also behind the forward limit, so the minimum fuel is used. For weight and balance purposes, the minimum fuel is no more than the quantity needed for one-half hour of operation at rated maximum continuous power. This is considered to be $\frac{1}{12}$ gallon for each maximum except takeoff (METO) horsepower. Because aviation gasoline weighs 6 pounds per gallon, determine the number of pounds of the minimum fuel by dividing the METO horsepower by two. In this example, minimum fuel is 115 pounds. The front and rear seats and the baggage are all behind the forward CG limit, so no passengers or baggage are considered.

Make a chart like the one in *Figure 7-9* to determine the CG with the aircraft loaded for its most forward CG. With the load consisting of only a pilot and the minimum fuel, the CG is +36.6, which is behind the most forward allowable limit for this weight of +33.0.

Aft Adverse-Load CG Check

To conduct an aft or rearward CG check, make a chart that includes the empty weight and EWCG of the aircraft after the alteration and all occupants and items of the load behind the aft CG limit of 46.0. The pilot is in front of this limit but is essential for flight and must be included. In this example, only the pilot occupies the front seats. Since the CG of the fuel is behind the aft limit, full fuel is used, as well as the nominal weight (170 lb) for both rear seat passengers and the maximum allowable baggage.

Under these loading conditions, the CG is located at +45.8, which is ahead of the aft limit of +46.0. [Figure 7-10] With only the pilot in front of the aft CG limit and maximum of all items behind the aft limit, the CG is at +45.8 inches, which is ahead of the aft limit of +46.0 inches.

Ballast

It is possible to load most modern airplanes so the CG shifts outside of the allowable limit. Placards and loading instructions in the weight and balance data inform the pilot of the restrictions that prevent such a shift from occurring. A typical placard in the baggage compartment of an airplane is shown in *Figure 7-11*. When the CG of an aircraft falls outside of the limits, it can usually be brought back in by using ballast.

> When rear row of seats is occupied, 120 pounds of baggage or ballast must be carried in forward baggage compartment. For additional loading instruction, see Weight and Balance Data.

Figure 7-11. *Typical baggage compartment placard.*

Item	Weight (lb)	X	Arm (in)	=	Moment (lb-in)	Most forward CG +33.0
Airplane (empty)	1,876.0		36.14		67,798.6	
Pilot	170.0		34.0		5,780.0	
Fuel (minimum)	115.0		48.0		5,520.0	
Total	2,161.0				79,098.6	+36.6

Figure 7-9. *Load conditions for forward adverse-load CG check.*

Item	Weight (lb)	X	Arm (in)	=	Moment (lb-in)	Most Aft CG +46.0
Airplane (empty)	1,876.0		36.14		67,798.6	
Pilot	170.0		34.0		5,780.0	
Fuel (full tanks – 88 gal)	528.0		48.2		25,449.6	
Rear seat occupants (2)	340.0		74.0		25,160.0	
Baggage A	100.0		97.0		9,700.0	
Baggage B	60.0		116.0		6,960.0	
Total	3,074.0				140,848.2	+45.8

Figure 7-10. *Load conditions for aft adverse-load CG check.*

Temporary Ballast

Temporary ballast, in the form of lead bars or heavy canvas bags of sand or lead shot, is often carried in the baggage compartments to adjust the balance for certain flight conditions. The bags are marked "Ballast XX Pounds— Removal Requires Weight and Balance Check." Temporary ballast must be secured so it cannot shift its location in flight, and the structural limits of the baggage compartment must not be exceeded. All temporary ballast must be removed before the aircraft is weighed.

Temporary Ballast Formula

The CG of a loaded airplane can be moved into its allowable range by shifting passengers or cargo or by adding temporary ballast.

Permanent Ballast

If a repair or alteration causes the aircraft CG to fall outside of its limit, permanent ballast can be installed. Usually permanent ballast is made of blocks of lead painted red and marked "Permanent Ballast—Do Not Remove." It should be attached to the structure so that it does not interfere with any control action and attached rigidly enough that it cannot be dislodged by any flight maneuvers or rough landing.

Two things must first be known to determine the amount of ballast needed to bring the CG within limits: the amount the CG is out of limits, and the distance between the location of the ballast and the limit that is affected.

If an airplane with an empty weight of 1,876 pounds has been altered so its EWCG is +32.2, and CG range for weights up to 2,250 pounds is +33.0 to +46.0, permanent ballast must be installed to move the EWCG from +32.2 to +33.0. There is a bulkhead at fuselage station 228 strong enough to support the ballast.

To determine the amount of ballast needed, use the formula in *Figure 7-13*.

$$\text{Ballast weight} = \frac{\text{Aircraft empty weight} \times \text{Dist. out of limits}}{\text{Distance between ballast and desired CG}}$$

Figure 7-13. *Formula for determining ballast.*

$$\text{Ballast needed} = \frac{1.876 \times 0.8}{228 - 33}$$

$$= \frac{1500.8}{195}$$

$$= 7.7 \text{ pounds}$$

A block of lead weighing 7.7 pounds, attached to the bulkhead at fuselage station 228, moves the EWCG back to its proper forward limit of +33. This block should be painted red and marked "Permanent Ballast—Do Not Remove."

Chapter 8
Weight and Balance Control—Helicopter

Introduction

Weight and balance considerations of a helicopter are similar to those of an airplane, except they are far more critical, and the center of gravity (CG) range is much more limited. *[Figures 8-1 and 8-2]* The engineers who design a helicopter determine the amount of cyclic control authority that is available, and establish both the longitudinal and lateral CG envelopes that allow the pilot to load the helicopter so there is sufficient cyclic control for all flight conditions.

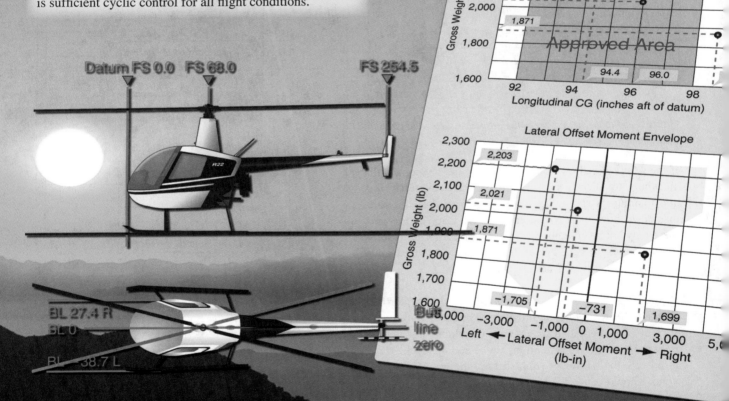

Item	Weight	X	Longitude Arm	=	Longitude Moment	Longitude CG	Weight	X	Latitude Arm	=	Lateral Offset Moment
Helicopter empty weight	1,545		101.4		156,663		1,545		+0.2		309
Pilot	200		64.0		12,800		200		+13.5		+2,700
Ballast/Passenger	150		64.0		9,600		150		−13.5		−2,025
Fuel (26 gallons)	156		96.0		14,976		156		−8.4		−1,310
	2,021				194,039	96.0	2,021				−731

Helicopter basic empty weight	1,545.0 lb, EWCG +101.4 (+0.2 lateral offset)
CG range	(+92.0) to (+98.0) at 1,600 lb (+92.0) to (+95.0) at 2,250 lb
Empty weight CG range	None
Maximum weight	2,250 lb
Number of seats	2 at (+64.0) (L–13.5) (R+13.5) lateral offset
Maximum baggage	(100 lb) at +105.0 (0.0 lateral offset)
Fuel capacity	50 gal (48 gal usable); 288 lb at (+96.0) (−8.4 lateral offset)
Oil capacity	4.3 qt at (+90) (0.0 lateral)

Figure 8-1. *Weight and balance data needed to determine proper loading of a helicopter.*

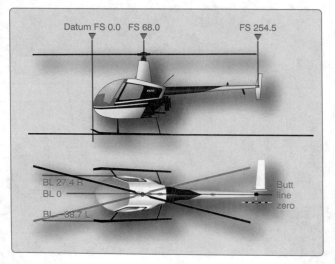

Figure 8-2. *Typical helicopter datum, flight stations, and butt line locations.*

If the CG is ahead of the forward limit, the helicopter tilts and the rotor disk has a forward pull. To counteract this and maintain a stationary position, rearward cyclic stick displacement would be required. If the CG is too far forward, there may not be enough available cyclic authority to allow the helicopter to flare during landing, and it consequently requires an excessive landing distance.

If the CG is aft of the allowable limits, the helicopter flies with a tail-low attitude and may need more forward cyclic stick displacement than is available to maintain a hover in a no-wind condition. There might not be enough cyclic travel to prevent the tail boom from striking the ground. If gusty winds should cause the helicopter to pitch up during high speed flight, there might not be enough forward cyclic control to safely lower the nose.

Helicopters are approved for a specific maximum gross weight, but it is not safe to operate them at this weight under some conditions. A high density altitude decreases the safe maximum weight as it affects the hovering, takeoff, climb, autorotation, and landing performance.

The fuel tanks on some helicopters are behind the CG, causing it to shift forward as fuel is used. Under some flight conditions, the balance may shift enough that there is not sufficient cyclic authority to flare for landing. For these helicopters, the loaded CG should be computed for both takeoff and landing weights.

Lateral balance of an airplane is usually of little concern and is not normally calculated. Some helicopters, especially those equipped for hoist operations, are sensitive to the lateral position of the CG and their Pilot's Operating Handbook/ Rotorcraft Flight Manual (POH/RFM) include both longitudinal and lateral CG envelopes, as well as information on the maximum permissible hoist load. *Figure 8-3* is an example of such CG envelopes.

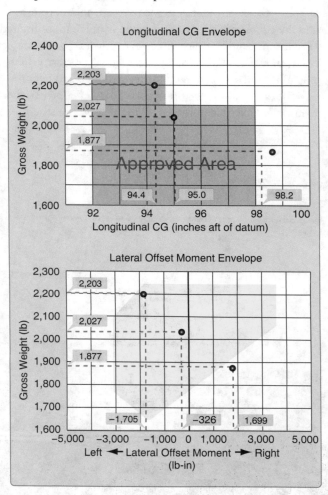

Figure 8-3. *Typical helicopter CG envelopes.*

Determining the Loaded CG of a Helicopter

The empty weight and empty weight center of gravity (EWCG) of a helicopter are determined in the same way as for an airplane. See Chapter 5, Single-Engine Aircraft Weight and Balance Computations. The weights recorded on the scales supporting the helicopter are added and their distances from the datum are used to compute the moments at each weighing point. The total moment is divided by the total weight to determine the location of the CG in inches from the datum. The datum of some helicopters is located at the center of the rotor mast, but since this causes some arms to be positive (behind the datum) and others negative (ahead of the datum), most modern helicopters have the datum located ahead of the aircraft, as do most modern airplanes. When the datum is ahead of the aircraft, all longitudinal arms are positive.

The lateral CG is determined in the same way as the longitudinal CG, except the distances between the scales and butt line zero (BL 0) are used as the arms. Arms to the right of BL 0 are positive and those to the left are negative. The butt line zero (or sometimes referred to as the buttock) is a line through the symmetrical center of an aircraft from nose to tail. It serves as the datum for measuring the arms used to find the lateral CG. Lateral moments that cause the aircraft to roll clockwise are positive (+), and those that cause it to roll counterclockwise are negative (−).

To determine whether or not a helicopter is within both longitudinal and lateral weight and balance limits, construct a table like the one in *Figure 8-4*, with the following data specific to the aircraft:

Empty weight...................................... 1,545 lb

EWCG.. 101.4 inches aft of the datum

Lateral balance.................................. arm 0.2 inches right of BL 0

Maximum allowable gross weight..... 2,250 lb

Pilot.. 200 lb @ 64 inches aft of datum and 13.5 inches right of BL 0

Passenger .... 170 lb @ 64 inches aft of datum and −13.5 in left of BL 0

Fuel (48 gal)...................................... 288 lb @ 96 inches aft of datum and −8.4 inches left of BL 0

Check the helicopter CG envelopes in *Figure 8-3* to determine whether or not the CG is within limits both longitudinally and laterally.

In the longitudinal CG envelope, draw a line vertically upward from the CG of 94.4 inches aft of datum and a horizontal line from the weight of 2,203 pounds gross weight. These lines cross within the approved area.

In the lateral offset moment envelope, draw a line vertically upward from the −1,705 lb-in point (on the left side of the horizontal axis) and a line horizontally from 2,203 pounds on the gross weight index. These lines cross within the envelope, showing the lateral balance is also within limits.

Effects of Offloading Passengers and Using Fuel

Consider the helicopter in *Figure 8-4*. The first leg of the flight consumes 26 gallons of fuel, and at the end of this leg, the passenger deplanes. Is the helicopter still within allowable CG limits for takeoff? To find out, make a new chart like the one in *Figure 8-5* to show the new loading conditions of the helicopter at the beginning of the second leg of the flight.

Under these conditions, according to the helicopter CG envelopes in *Figure 8-3*, both the longitudinal CG and the lateral offset moment fall outside of the approved area of the envelope. The aircraft longitudinal CG is too far aft and the potential for excessive tail-low attitudes is very high. Under these conditions, it is possible that there will not be enough forward cyclic authority to maintain level flight. The helicopter's lateral offset moment is too far right and may lead to control issues, as well as an increased hazard of dynamic rollover. One possible option to bring the aircraft loading conditions within the approved envelope is to load either ballast or a passenger, as computed in *Figure 8-6* and plotted in *Figure 8-3*.

Item	Weight	X	Longitude Arm	=	Longitude Moment	Longitude CG	Weight	X	Latitude Arm	=	Lateral Offset Moment
Helicopter empty weight	1,545		101.4		156,663		1,545		+0.2		309
Pilot	200		64.0		12,800		200		+13.5		+2,700
Passenger	170		64.0		10,880		170		–13.5		–2,295
Fuel (48 gallons)	288		96.0		27,648		288		–8.4		–2,419
	2,203				207,991	94.4	2,203				–1,705

Figure 8-4. *Determining the longitudinal CG and the lateral offset moment.*

Item	Weight	X	Longitude Arm	=	Longitude Moment	Longitude CG	Weight	X	Latitude Arm	=	Lateral Offset Moment
Helicopter empty weight	1,545		101.4		156,663		1,545		+0.2		309
Pilot	200		64.0		12,800		200		+13.5		+2,700
Fuel (22 gallons)	132		96.0		14,976		132		–8.4		–1,310
	1,877				184,439	98.2	1,877				+1,699

Figure 8-5. *Determining the longitudinal CG and the lateral offset moment for the second leg of the flight.*

Item	Weight	X	Longitude Arm	=	Longitude Moment	Longitude CG	Weight	X	Latitude Arm	=	Lateral Offset Moment
Helicopter empty weight	1,545		101.4		156,663		1,545		+0.2		309
Pilot	200		64.0		12,800		200		+13.5		+2,700
Ballast/Passenger	150		64.0		9,600		150		–13.5		–2,025
Fuel (22 gallons)	132		96.0		14,976		132		–8.4		–1,310
	2,027				194,039	95.0	2,027				–731

Figure 8-6. *Determining the longitudinal CG and the lateral offset moment for the second leg of the flight with ballast and/or a different passenger.*

Weight and Balance Control— Commuter Category and Large Aircraft

Introduction

This chapter discusses general guidelines and procedures for weighing large fixed-wing aircraft exceeding a takeoff weight of 12,500 pounds. Several examples of center of gravity (CG) determination for various operational aspects of these aircraft are also included. Persons seeking approval for a weight and balance control program for aircraft operated under Title 14 of the Code of Federal Regulations (14 CFR) part 91, subpart K, 121, 125, or 135 should consult with the Flight Standards District Office (FSDO) or Certificate Management Office (CMO) that has jurisdiction in their area. Additional information on weight and balance for large aircraft can be found in Federal Aviation Administration (FAA) Advisory Circular (AC) 120-27, Aircraft Weight and Balance Control, FAA Type Certificate Data Sheets (TCDS), and the aircraft flight and maintenance manuals for specific aircraft.

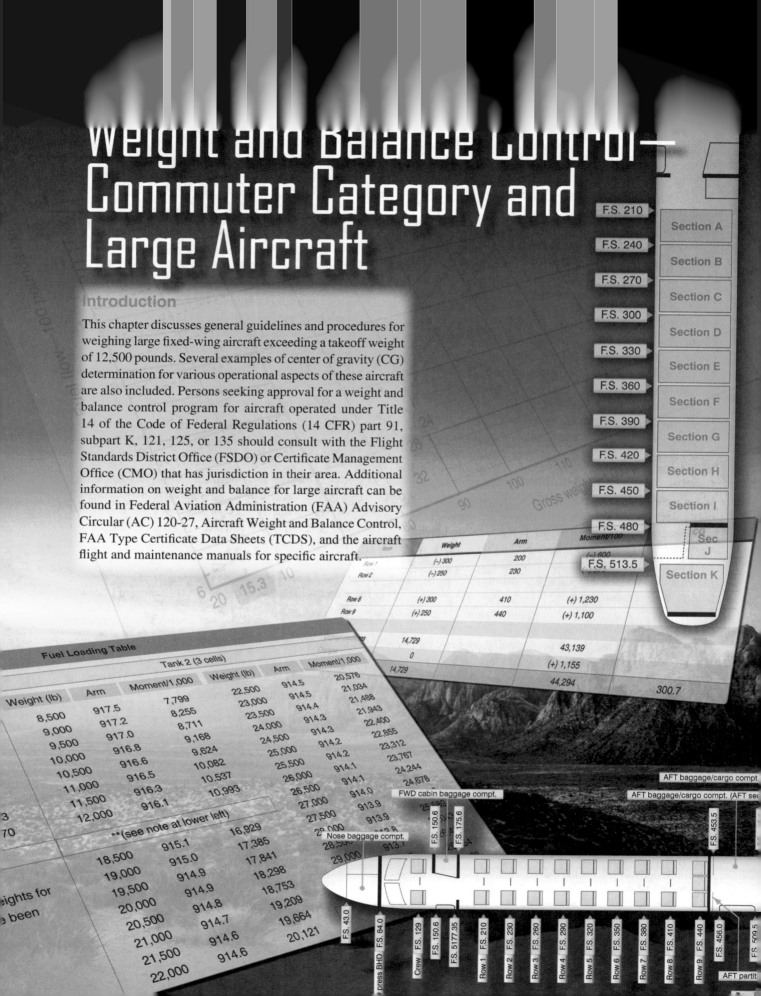

F.S. 210	Section A
F.S. 240	Section B
F.S. 270	Section C
F.S. 300	Section D
F.S. 330	Section E
F.S. 360	Section F
F.S. 390	Section G
F.S. 420	Section H
F.S. 450	Section I
F.S. 480	Sec J
F.S. 513.5	Section K

Item	Weight	Arm	Moment/100
Row 1	(−) 300	200	(−) 600
Row 2	(−) 250	230	
Row 8	(+) 300	410	(+) 1,230
Row 9	(+) 250	440	(+) 1,100
	14,729		43,139
	0		(+) 1,155
14,729			44,294	300.7

Fuel Loading Table

			Tank 2 (3 cells)		
Weight (lb)	Arm	Moment/1,000	Weight (lb)	Arm	Moment/1,000
8,500	917.5	7,799	22,500	914.5	20,576
9,000	917.2	8,255	23,000	914.5	21,034
9,500	917.0	8,711	23,500	914.4	21,488
10,000	916.8	9,168	24,000	914.3	21,943
10,500	916.6	9,624	24,500	914.3	22,400
11,000	916.5	10,082	25,000	914.2	22,855
11,500	916.3	10,537	25,500	914.2	23,312
12,000	916.1	10,993	26,000	914.1	23,767
			26,500	914.1	24,244
	**(see note at lower left)		27,000	914.0	24,878
		16,929	27,500	913.9	
18,500	915.1	17,385	28,000	913.9	
19,000	915.0	17,841	28,500	913.8	
19,500	914.9	18,298	29,000	913.7	
20,000	914.9	18,753			
20,500	914.8	19,209			
21,000	914.7	19,664			
21,500	914.6	20,121			
22,000	914.6				

FWD cabin baggage compt.

Nose baggage compt.

AFT baggage/cargo compt.

AFT baggage/cargo compt. (AFT sec

F.S. 150.6 F.S. 175.6 F.S. 453.5

F.S. 43.0 F.S. 84.0 press BHD Crew F.S. 129 F.S. 150.6 F.S. 5177.35 Row 1 F.S. 210 Row 2 F.S. 230 Row 3 F.S. 260 Row 4 F.S. 290 Row 5 F.S. 320 Row 6 F.S. 350 Row 7 F.S. 380 Row 8 F.S. 410 Row 9 F.S. 440 F.S. 456.0 F.S. 500.5

AFT partit

Establishing the Initial Weight of an Aircraft

Prior to being placed into service, each aircraft is weighed and the empty weight and CG location established. New aircraft are normally weighed at the factory and are eligible to be placed into operation without reweighing if the weight and balance records were adjusted for alterations and modifications to the aircraft, such as interior reconfigurations.

An aircraft transferred from one operator that has an approved weight and balance program to another operator with an approved program does not need to be weighed prior to use by the receiving operator unless more than 36 calendar months have elapsed since the last individual or fleet weighing, or unless some other modification to the aircraft warrants that the aircraft be weighed. Aircraft transferred, purchased, or leased from an operator without an approved weight and balance program, and that have not been modified or have been minimally modified, can be placed into service without being reweighed if the last weighing was accomplished by an acceptable method (for example, manufacturer's instructions or AC 43.13-2, Acceptable Methods, Techniques, and Practices—Aircraft Alterations) within the last 12 calendar months and a weight and balance change record was maintained by the operator. It is potentially unsafe to fail to reweigh an aircraft after it has been modified.

When weighing large aircraft, compliance with the relevant manuals, operations specifications, or management specification is required to ensure that weight and balance requirements specified in the Aircraft Flight Manual (AFM) are met in accordance with approved limits. This provides information to the flight crew that allows the maximum payload to be carried safely.

The aircraft should be weighed in still air or an enclosed building after the aircraft has been cleaned. Ensure that the aircraft is in a configuration for weighing with regard to flight controls, unusable fuel, ballast, oil and other operating fluids, and equipment as required by the controlling weight and balance procedure.

Large aircraft are not usually raised off the floor on jacks for weighing; they are weighed on ramp-type scales. The scales must be properly calibrated, zeroed, and used in accordance with the manufacturer's instructions. Each scale should be periodically checked for accuracy as recommended in the manufacturer's calibration schedule, either by the manufacturer or by a recognized facility, such as a civil department of weights and measures. If no manufacturer's schedule is available, the period between calibrations should not exceed 12 months.

Determining the Empty Weight and Empty Weight CG (EWCG)

When the aircraft is properly prepared for weighing, roll it onto the scales, and level it. The weights are measured at three weighing points: the two main wheel points and the nosewheel point. The empty weight and empty weight CG (EWCG) are determined by using the following steps with the results recorded in the weight and balance record for use in all future weight and balance computations.

1. Determine the moment index of each of the main-wheel points by multiplying the net weight (scale reading minus tare weight), in pounds, at these points by the distance from the datum, in inches. Divide these numbers by the appropriate reduction factor.

2. Determine the moment index of the nosewheel weighing point by multiplying its net weight, in pounds, by its distance from the datum, in inches. Divide this by the reduction factor.

3. Determine the total weight by adding the net weight of the three weighing points and the total moment index by adding the moment indexes of each point.

4. Divide the total moment index by the total weight and multiply the result by the reduction factor. This gives the CG in inches from the datum.

5. Determine the distance of the CG behind the leading edge of the mean aerodynamic chord (LEMAC) by subtracting the distance between the datum and LEMAC from the distance between the datum and the CG. [Figure 9-1]

Distance CG to LEMAC = Datum to CG – Datum to LEMAC

Figure 9-1. *Determining the distance of CG.*

6. Determine the EWCG in percentage of MAC (percent MAC) by using the formula in *Figure 9-2.*

$$\text{EWCG in \% MAC} = \frac{\text{CG in inches from LEMAC} \times 100}{\text{MAC}}$$

Figure 9-2. *Determining the EWCG in percent MAC.*

In the weight change record of a—	An operator should record any weight changes of—
Large cabin aircraft	± 10 lb or greater
Medium cabin aircraft	± 5 lb or greater
Small cabin aircraft	± 1 lb or greater

Figure 9-3. *Incremental weight changes that should be recorded in a weight and balance change record.*

Documenting Changes to an Aircraft's Weight and Balance

The weight and balance system should include methods by which a complete, current, and continuous record of the weight and CG of each aircraft is maintained, such as a log, ledger, or other equivalent electronic means. Alterations and changes affecting the weight and/or balance of the aircraft should be recorded in this log. Changes in the weight or location of weight in or on the aircraft should be recorded whenever the weight change is at or exceeds the weights listed in *Figure 9-3*.

Determining the Loaded CG of the Airplane in Percent MAC

A loading schedule is used to document compliance with the certificated weight and balance limitations contained in the manufacturer's AFM and weight and balance manual. The basic operating weight (BOW) and the operating index are entered into a loading schedule like the one in *Figure 9-4*, and the variables for a specific flight are entered as appropriate to determine the loaded weight and CG.

Use the data in this example:

Basic operating weight .... 105,500 lb

Basic operating index (total moment/1,000) 98,837.0

MAC .... 180.9 in

LEMAC 860.5

Item	Weight (lb)	Moment/1,000
BOW	105,500	92,837
Passengers Fwd station	3,060	1,781
Passengers Aft station	16,150	16,602
Fwd cargo	1,500	1,020
Aft cargo	2,500	2,915
Fuel tank 1	10,500	10,451
Fuel tank 3	10,500	10,451
Fuel tank 2	28,000	25,589
	177,710	161,646

Figure 9-4. *Loading schedule.*

Figure 9-5 illustrates passenger, cargo, and fuel loading tables. Using these tables, determine the moment indexes for the passengers (PAX), cargo, and fuel.

The airplane is loaded in this way:

Passengers (nominal weight—170 pounds each)

Forward compartment 18

Aft compartment 95

Cargo

Forward hold .... 1,500 lb

Aft hold .... 2,500 lb

Fuel

Tanks 1 and 3 .... 10,500 lb each

Tank 2 .... 28,000 lb

The formula in *Figure 9-6* can be used to determine the location of the CG in inches aft of the datum.

Passenger Loading Table

# of passengers	Weight (lb)	Moment/1,000
Forward compartment centroid—582.0		
5	850	495
10	1,700	989
15	2,550	1,484
20	3,400	1,979
25	4,250	2,473
29	4,930	2,869
Aft compartment centroid—1,028.0		
10	1,700	1,748
20	3,400	3,495
30	5,100	5,243
40	6,800	6,990
50	8,500	8,738
60	10,200	10,486
70	11,900	12,233
80	13,600	13,980
90	15,300	15,728
100	17,000	17,476
110	18,700	19,223
120	20,400	20,971
133	22,610	23,243

Cargo Loading Table

	Moment/1,000	
Weight (lb)	Forward hold arm—680.0	Aft hold arm—1,166.0
6,000		6,966
5,000	3,400	5,830
4,000	2,720	4,664
3,000	2,040	3,498
2,000	1,360	2,332
1,000	680	1,166
900	612	1,049
800	544	933
700	476	816
600	408	700
500	340	583
400	272	466
300	204	350
200	136	233
100	68	117

Fuel Loading Table

Tanks 1 and 3 (each)

Weight (lb)	Arm	Moment/1,000
8,500	992.1	8,433
9,000	993.0	8,937
9,500	993.9	9,442
10,000	994.7	9,947
10,500	995.4	10,451
11,000	996.1	10,957
11,500	996.8	11,463
12,000	997.5	11,970
Full capacity		

** Note:
Computations for Tank 2 weights for 12,500 lb to 18,000 lb have been purposely omitted.

Tank 2 (3 cells)

Weight (lb)	Arm	Moment/1,000	Weight (lb)	Arm	Moment/1,000
8,500	917.5	7,799	22,500	914.5	20,576
9,000	917.2	8,255	23,000	914.5	21,034
9,500	917.0	8,711	23,500	914.4	21,488
10,000	916.8	9,168	24.000	914.3	21,943
10,500	916.6	9,624	24,500	914.3	22,400
11,000	916.5	10,082	25,000	914.2	22,855
11,500	916.3	10.537	25,500	914.2	23,312
12,000	916.1	10,993	26,000	914.1	23,767
**(see note at lower left)			26,500	914.1	24,244
18,500	915.1	16,929	27,000	914.0	24,678
19,000	915.0	17,385	27,500	913.9	25,132
19,500	914.9	17,841	28,000	913.9	25,589
20,000	914.9	18,298	28,500	913.8	26,043
20,500	914.8	18,753	29,000	913.7	26,497
21,000	914.7	19,209	29,500	913.7	26,954
21,500	914.6	19,664	30,000	913.6	27,408
22,000	914.6	20,121	**Full capacity**		

Figure 9-5. *Loading schedule for determining weight and CG.*

$$\text{CG inches aft of datum} = \left(\frac{\text{Total moment index}}{\text{Total weight}}\right) \times 1{,}000$$

$$= \left(\frac{161{,}646}{177{,}710}\right) \times 1{,}000$$

$$= 909.6 \text{ inches}$$

Figure 9-6. *Determining the location of the CG in inches aft of the datum.*

Determine the distance from the CG to the LEMAC by subtracting the distance between the datum and LEMAC from the distance between the datum and the CG. *[Figure 9-7]*

$$\text{Distance CG to LEMAC} = \text{Datum to CG} - \text{Datum to LEMAC}$$

$$= 909.6 - 860.5$$

$$= 49.1 \text{ inches}$$

Figure 9-7. *Determining the distance from the CG to the LEMAC.*

The location of the CG in percent MAC must be known in order to set the stabilizer trim takeoff. *[Figure 9-8]*

$$\text{CG \% MAC} = \left(\frac{\text{Distance CG to LEMAC}}{\text{MAC}}\right) \times 100$$

$$= \left(\frac{49.1}{180.9}\right) \times 100$$

$$= 27.1\%$$

Figure 9-8. *Determining the location of the CG in percent MAC.*

Operational Empty Weight (OEW)

Operational empty weight (OEW) is the basic empty weight or fleet empty weight plus operational items. The operator has two choices for maintaining OEW. The loading schedule may be utilized to compute the operational weight and balance of an individual aircraft, or the operator may choose to establish fleet empty weights for a fleet or group of aircraft.

Reestablishing the OEW

The OEW and CG position of each aircraft should be reestablished at the reweighing. In addition, it should be reestablished through calculation whenever the cumulative change to the weight and balance log is more than plus or minus one-half of 1 percent (0.5 percent) of the maximum landing weight, or whenever the cumulative change in the CG position exceeds one-half of 1 percent (0.5 percent) of the MAC. In the case of rotorcraft and aircraft that do not have a

MAC-based CG envelope (e.g., canard equipped airplane), whenever the cumulative change in the CG position exceeds one-half of 1 percent (0.5 percent) of the total CG range, the weight and balance should be reestablished.

When reestablishing the aircraft OEW between reweighing periods, the weight changes may be computed provided the weight and CG location of the modifications are known; otherwise, the aircraft must be reweighed.

Fleet Operating Empty Weights (FOEW)

An operator may choose to use one weight for a fleet or group of aircraft if the weight and CG of each aircraft is within the limits stated above for establishment of OEW. When the cumulative changes to an aircraft weight and balance log exceed the weight or CG limits for the established fleet weight, the empty weight for that aircraft should be reestablished. This may be done by moving the aircraft to another group, or reestablishing new fleet operating empty weights (FOEWs).

Onboard Aircraft Weighing System

Some large transport airplanes have an onboard aircraft weighing system (OBAWS) that, when the aircraft is on the ground, gives the flight crew a continuous indication of the aircraft total weight and the location of the CG in percent MAC. Procedures are required to ensure the onboard weight and balance system equipment is periodically calibrated in accordance with the manufacturer's instructions.

An operator may use an onboard weight and balance system to measure an aircraft's weight and balance as a primary means to dispatch an aircraft, provided the FAA has certified the system and approved the system for use in an operator's weight and balance control program. As part of the approval process, the onboard weight and balance system must maintain its certificated accuracy. The accuracy demonstration test is provided in the maintenance manual portion of the Supplemental Type Certificate (STC) or type certificate of the onboard weight and balance system.

The system consists of strain-sensing transducers in each main wheel and nosewheel axle, a weight and balance computer, and indicators that show the gross weight, the CG location in percent MAC, and an indicator of the ground attitude of the aircraft.

The strain sensors measure the amount each axle deflects and sends this data into the computer, where signals from all of the transducers and the ground attitude sensor are integrated. The results are displayed on the indicators for the flight crew. Using an onboard weight and balance system does not relieve an operator from the requirement to complete and maintain a load manifest.

Determining the Correct Stabilizer Trim Setting

It is important before takeoff to set the stabilizer trim for the existing CG location. There are two ways the stabilizer trim setting systems may be calibrated: in percent MAC and in units airplane nose up (ANU).

If the stabilizer trim is calibrated in percent MAC, determine the CG location in percent MAC as has just been described, then set the stabilizer trim on the percentage figure thus determined. Some aircraft give the stabilizer trim setting in units of ANU that correspond with the location of the CG in percent MAC. When preparing for takeoff in an aircraft equipped with this system, first determine the CG in percent MAC in the way described above, then refer to the stabilizer trim setting chart on the takeoff performance page of the pertinent AFM. *Figure 9-9* is an excerpt from the AFM chart on the takeoff performance of a Boeing 737.

Stabilizer Trim Setting—Units Airplane Nose Up	
CG	**Flaps (all)**
6	8
8	7¾
10	7½
12	7
14	6¾
16	6¼
18	5¾
20	5½
22	5
24	4½
26	4
28	3½
30	3
32	2½

Figure 9-9. *Stabilizer trim setting in ANU units.*

Consider an airplane with these specifications:

CG location.. station 635.7

LEMAC .... station 625

MAC... 134.0 in

1. Determine the distance from the CG to the LEMAC by using the formula in *Figure 9-10*.

2. Determine the location of the CG in percent MAC by using the formula found in *Figure 9-11*.

Refer to *Figure 9-9* for all flap settings and a CG located at 8 percent MAC; the stabilizer setting is 7¾ units ANU.

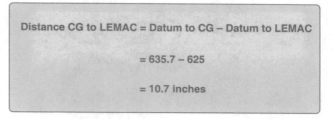

$$\text{Distance CG to LEMAC} = \text{Datum to CG} - \text{Datum to LEMAC}$$
$$= 635.7 - 625$$
$$= 10.7 \text{ inches}$$

Figure 9-10. *Determining the distance from CG to the LEMAC.*

$$\text{CG in \% MAC} = \left(\frac{\text{Distance CG to LEMAC}}{\text{MAC}}\right) \times 100$$
$$= \left(\frac{10.7}{134.0}\right) \times 100$$
$$= 8.0 \text{ \% MAC}$$

Figure 9-11. *Determining the location of CG in percent MAC.*

Determining CG Changes Caused by Modifying the Cargo

Since large aircraft can carry substantial cargo, adding, subtracting, or moving any of the cargo from one hold to another can cause large shifts in the CG.

Effects of Loading or Offloading Cargo

Both the weight and CG of an aircraft are changed when cargo is loaded or offloaded. In the following example, the new weight and CG are calculated after 2,500 pounds of cargo is offloaded from the forward cargo hold.

Aircraft specifications are:

Loaded weight ....90,000 lb

Loaded CG... 22.5 percent MAC

Weight change ....2,500 lb

Forward cargo hold centroid...................... station 352.1

MAC ....141.5 in

LEMAC .... station 549.13

1. Determine the CG location in inches from the datum before the cargo is removed. Do this by first determining the distance of the CG aft of the LEMAC. *[Figure 9-12]*

$$\text{CG (inches aft of LEMAC)} = \left(\frac{\text{CG in \% MAC}}{100}\right) \times \text{MAC}$$
$$= \left(\frac{22.5}{100}\right) \times 141.5$$
$$= 31.84 \text{ inches}$$

Figure 9-12. *Determining the location of CG in inches before cargo is removed.*

2. Determine the distance between the CG and the datum by adding the CG in inches aft of LEMAC to the distance from the datum to LEMAC. *[Figure 9-13]*

$$CG \text{ (inches from datum)} = CG \text{ inches aft of LEMAC} + \text{Datum to LEMAC}$$

$$= 31.84 + 549.13$$

$$= 580.97 \text{ inches}$$

Figure 9-13. *Determining the distance between CG and the datum.*

3. Determine the moment/1,000 for the original weight. *[Figure 9-14]*

$$\text{Moment/1,000} = \frac{\text{Weight} \times \text{Arm}}{1,000}$$

$$= \frac{90,000 \times 580.97}{1,000}$$

$$= 52,287.3$$

Figure 9-14. *Determining the moment/1,000 for the original weight.*

4. Determine the new weight and new CG by first determining the moment/1,000 of the removed weight. Multiply the weight removed (2,500 pounds) by the centroid of the forward cargo hold (352.1 inches), and then divide the result by 1,000. *[Figure 9-15]*

$$\text{Moment/1,000} = \frac{\text{Weight} \times \text{Arm}}{1,000}$$

$$= \frac{2,500 \times 352.1}{1,000}$$

$$= 880.25$$

Figure 9-15. *Determining the moment/1,000 of the removed weight.*

5. Subtract the removed weight from the original weight and subtract the moment/1,000 of the removed weight from the original moment/1,000. *[Figure 9-16]*

6. Determine the location of the new CG by dividing the total moment/1,000 by the total weight and multiplying this by the reduction factor of 1,000. *[Figure 9-17]*

$$CG = \frac{\text{Total moment/1,000}}{\text{Total weight}} \times 1,000$$

$$= \frac{51,407.0}{87,500} \times 1,000$$

$$= 587.51 \text{ inches behind the datum}$$

Figure 9-17. *Determining the location of new CG.*

7. Convert the new CG location to percent MAC. First, determine the distance between the CG location and LEMAC. *[Figure 9-18]*

$$CG \text{ (inches aft of LEMAC)} = CG \text{ (inches from datum)} - LEMAC$$

$$= 587.51 - 549.13$$

$$= 38.38 \text{ inches}$$

Figure 9-18. *Determining the distance between the CG and LEMAC.*

8. Then, determine the new CG in percent MAC. *[Figure 9-19]*

$$CG \text{ \% MAC} = \left(\frac{\text{Distance CG to LEMA}}{\text{MAC}} \right) \times 100$$

$$= \left(\frac{38.38}{141.5} \right) \times 100$$

$$= 27.12\% \text{ MAC}$$

Figure 9-19. *Determining the new CG in percent MAC.*

Loading 3,000 pounds of cargo into the forward cargo hold moves the CG forward 5.51 inches, from 27.12 percent MAC to 21.59 percent MAC.

	Weight (lb)	Moment/1,000	CG (inches from datum)	CG (percent MAC)
Original data	90,000	52,287.3	580.97	22.5
Changes	− 2,500	− 880.3		
New data	87,500	51,407.0	587.51	27.12

Figure 9-16. *New weights and CG.*

Effects of Shifting Cargo From One Hold to Another

When cargo is shifted from one cargo hold to another, the CG changes, but the total weight of the aircraft remains the same.

For example, use the following data:

Loaded weight .... 90,000 lb

Loaded CG............. station 580.97 (22.5 percent MAC)

Forward cargo hold centroid........................ station 352

Aft cargo hold centroid........................... station 724.9

MAC .... 141.5 in

LEMAC .... station 549

To determine the change in CG (ΔCG) caused by shifting 2,500 pounds of cargo from the forward cargo hold to the aft cargo hold, use the formula in *Figure 9-20*.

$$\Delta CG = \frac{\text{Weight shifted} \times \text{Distance shifted}}{\text{Total weight}}$$

$$= \frac{2{,}500 \times (724.9 - 352)}{90{,}000}$$

$$= \frac{2{,}500 \times 372.9}{90{,}000}$$

$$= 10.36 \text{ inches}$$

Figure 9-20. *Calculating the change in CG, using index arms.*

Since the weight was shifted aft, the CG moved aft and the CG change is positive. If the shift were forward, the CG change would be negative.

Before the cargo was shifted, the CG was located at station 580.97, which is 22.5 percent of MAC. The CG moved aft 10.36 inches, so the new CG is found using the formula from *Figure 9-21*.

$$\text{New CG} = \text{Old CG} \pm \Delta CG$$

$$= 580.97 + 10.36$$

$$= 591.33 \text{ inches}$$

Figure 9-21. *Determining the new CG after shifting cargo weight.*

Convert the location of the CG in inches aft of the datum to percent MAC by using the formula in *Figure 9-22*.

The new CG in percent MAC caused by shifting the cargo is the sum of the old CG plus the change in CG. *[Figure 9-23]*

$$\Delta CG \text{ \% MAC} = \left(\frac{\Delta CG \text{ inches}}{MAC}\right) \times 100$$

$$= \left(\frac{10.36}{141.5}\right) \times 100$$

$$= 7.32\% \text{ MAC}$$

Figure 9-22. *Converting the location of CG to percent MAC.*

$$\text{New CG \% MAC} = \text{Old CG} \pm \Delta CG$$

$$= 22.5\% + 7.32\%$$

$$= 29.82\% \text{ MAC}$$

Figure 9-23. *Determining the new CG in percent MAC.*

Some AFMs locate the CG relative to an index point rather than the datum or the MAC. An index point is a location specified by the aircraft manufacturer from which arms used in weight and balance computations are measured. Arms measured from the index point are called index arms, and objects ahead of the index point have negative index arms, while those behind the index point have positive index arms.

Use the same data as in the previous example, except for these changes:

Loaded CG.......................... index arm of 0.97, which is 22.5 percent of MAC

Index point.................................. fuselage station 580.0

Forward cargo hold centroid............... −227.9 index arm

Aft cargo hold centroid....................... +144.9 index arm

MAC .... 141.5 in

LEMAC .... −30.87 index arm

The weight was shifted 372.8 inches (−227.9 + Δ = +144.9, Δ = 372.8).

The change in CG can be calculated by using this formula found in *Figure 9-24*.

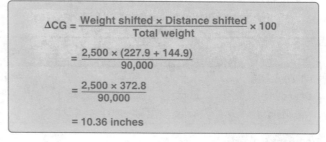

$$\Delta CG = \frac{\text{Weight shifted} \times \text{Distance shifted}}{\text{Total weight}} \times 100$$

$$= \frac{2{,}500 \times (227.9 + 144.9)}{90{,}000}$$

$$= \frac{2{,}500 \times 372.8}{90{,}000}$$

$$= 10.36 \text{ inches}$$

Figure 9-24. *Determining the change in CG caused by shifting 2,500 pounds of cargo.*

Since the weight was shifted aft, the CG moved aft, and the CG change is positive. If the shift were forward, the CG change would be negative. Before the cargo was shifted, the CG was located at 0.97 index arm, which is 22.5 percent MAC. The CG moved aft 10.36 inches, and the new CG is shown using the formula in *Figure 9-25*.

$$New\ CG = Old\ CG \pm \Delta CG$$
$$= 0.97 + 10.36$$
$$= 11.33\ index\ arm$$

Figure 9-25. *Determining the new CG, moved aft 10.36 inches.*

The change in the CG in percent MAC is determined by using the formula in *Figure 9-26*.

$$New\ CG\ \%\ MAC = Old\ CG \pm \Delta CG$$
$$= 22.5\% + 7.32\%$$
$$= 29.82\%\ MAC$$

Figure 9-26. *The change in the CG in percent MAC.*

The new CG in percent MAC is the sum of the old CG plus the change in CG. *[Figure 9-27]*

$$\Delta CG\ \%\ MAC = \left(\frac{\Delta CG\ inches}{MAC}\right) \times 100$$
$$= \left(\frac{10.36}{141.5}\right) \times 100$$
$$= 7.32\%\ MAC$$

Figure 9-27. *The new CG in percent MAC.*

Notice that the new CG is in the same location whether the distances are measured from the datum or from the index point.

Determining Cargo Pallet Loads and Floor Loading Limits

Each cargo hold has a structural floor loading limit based on the weight of the load and the area over which this weight is distributed. To determine the maximum weight of a loaded cargo pallet that can be carried in a cargo hold, divide its total weight, which includes the weight of the empty pallet and its tie down devices, by its area in square feet. This load per square foot must be equal to or less than the floor load limit.

In this example, determine the maximum load that can be placed on this pallet without exceeding the floor loading limit.

Pallet dimensions .... 36 by 48 in

Empty pallet weight .... 47 lb

Tie down devices .... 33 lb

Floor load limit .... 169 lb per square foot

The pallet has an area of 36 inches (3 feet) by 48 inches (4 feet), which equals 12 square feet, and the floor has a load limit of 169 pounds per square foot. Therefore, the total weight of the loaded pallet can be $169 \times 12 = 2,028$ pounds. Subtracting the weight of the pallet and the tie down devices gives an allowable load of 1,948 pounds (2,028 – [47 + 33]).

Determine the floor loading limit that is needed to carry a loaded cargo pallet having the following dimensions and weights:

Pallet dimensions .... 48.5 by 33.5 in

Pallet weight .... 44 lb

Tiedown devices .... 27 lb

Cargo weight .... 786.5 lb

First, determine the number of square feet of pallet area as

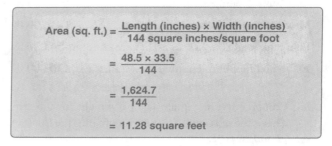

Figure 9-28. *Determining pallet area in square feet.*

shown in *Figure 9-28*.

Then, determine the total weight of the loaded pallet:

Pallet .... 44.0 lb

Tiedown devices .... 27.0 lb

Cargo .... 786.5 lb

Total... 857.5 lb

Determine the load imposed on the floor by the loaded pallet. *[Figure 9-29]* The floor must have a minimum loading limit of 76 pounds per square foot.

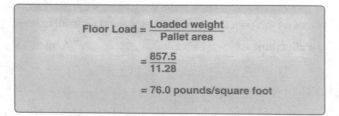

$$\text{Floor Load} = \frac{\text{Loaded weight}}{\text{Pallet area}}$$

$$= \frac{857.5}{11.28}$$

$$= 76.0 \text{ pounds/square foot}$$

Figure 9-29. *Determining the load imposed on the floor by the loaded pallet.*

Determining the Maximum Amount of Payload That Can Be Carried

The primary function of a transport or cargo aircraft is to carry payload, which is the portion of the useful load, passengers, or cargo that produces revenue. To determine the maximum amount of payload that can be carried, both the maximum limits for the aircraft and the trip limits imposed by the particular trip must be considered. In each of the following steps, the trip limit must be less than the maximum limit. If it is not, the maximum limit must be used.

These are the specifications for the aircraft in this example:

Basic operating weight (BOW) .... 100,500 lb

Maximum zero fuel weight............................ 138,000 lb

Maximum landing weight.............................. 142,000 lb

Maximum takeoff weight .... 184,200 lb

Fuel tank load .... 54,000 lb

Estimated fuel burn en route.......................... 40,000 lb

1. Compute the maximum takeoff weight for this trip. This is the maximum landing weight plus the trip fuel. *[Figure 9-30]*

Max limit		Trip limit
142,000	Landing weight	142,000
	+ trip fuel	+ 40,000
184,200	Takeoff weight	182,000

Figure 9-30. *Finding the maximum takeoff weight.*

2. The trip limit is lower than the maximum takeoff weight, so it is used to determine the zero fuel weight. *[Figure 9-31]*

Max limit		Trip limit
184,200	Landing weight	182,000
	– fuel load	– 54,000
138,000	Zero fuel weight	128,000

Figure 9-31. *Determining zero fuel weight with lower trip limits.*

3. The trip limit is again lower than the maximum takeoff weight, so use it to compute the maximum payload for this trip. *[Figure 9-32]*

Max limit		Trip limit
138,000	Zero fuel weight	128,000
	– BOW	–100,500
	Payload (pounds)	27,500

Figure 9-32. *Finding maximum payload with lower trip limits.*

Under these conditions, 27,500 pounds of payload may be carried.

Determining the Landing Weight

It is important to know the landing weight of the aircraft in order to set up the landing parameters and to be certain the aircraft is able to land safely at the intended destination.

In this example of a four-engine turboprop airplane, determine the airplane weight at the end of 4.0 hours of cruise under these conditions:

Takeoff weight... 140,000 lb

Pressure altitude during cruise........................... 16,000 ft

Ambient temperature during cruise .... –32 °C

Fuel burned during descent and landing........... 1,350 lb

Refer to the U.S. Standard Atmosphere Table in *Figure 9-33* and the gross weight table in *Figure 9-34* when completing the following steps:

1. Use the U.S. Standard Atmosphere Table to determine the standard temperature for 16,000 feet (–16.7 °C).

2. The ambient temperature is –32 °C, which is a deviation from standard of 15.3 °C. (–32° – (–16.7°) = –15.3°). It is below standard.

3. In the gross weight table, follow the vertical line representing 140,000 pounds gross weight upward until it intersects the diagonal line for 16,000 feet pressure altitude.

4. From this intersection, draw a horizontal line to the left to the temperature deviation index (0 °C deviation).

5. Draw a diagonal line parallel to the dashed lines for Below Standard from the intersection of the horizontal line and the Temperature Deviation Index.

6. Draw a vertical line upward from the 15.3 °C Temperature Deviation From Standard.

Feet	inHg	mmHg	PSI	°C	°F
0	29.92	760.0	14.7	15.0	59.0
2,000	27.82	706.7	13.66	11.0	51.9
4,000	25.84	656.3	12.69	7.1	44.7
6,000	23.98	609.1	11.78	3.1	37.6
8,000	22.23	564.6	10.92	−0.8	30.5
10,000	20.58	522.7	10.11	−0.4	23.3
12,000	19.03	483.4	9.35	−8.8	16.2
14,000	17.58	446.5	8.63	−12.7	9.1
16,000	16.22	412.0	7.96	−16.7	1.9
18,000	14.95	379.7	7.34	−20.7	−5.2
20,000	13.76	349.5	6.75	−24.6	−12.3
22,000	12.65	321.3	6.21	−28.6	−19.5
24,000	11.61	294.9	5.70	−32.5	−26.6
26,000	10.64	270.3	5.22	−36.5	−33.7
28,000	9.74	237.4	4.78	−40.4	−40.9
30,000	8.90	226.1	4.37	−44.4	−48.0
32,000	8.12	206.3	3.98	−48.4	−55.1
34,000	7.40	188.0	3.63	−52.4	−62.3
36,000	6.73	171.0	3.30	−56.3	−69.4
38,000	6.12	155.5	2.99	−56.5	−69.7
40,000	5.56	141.2	2.72	−56.5	−69.7
42,000	5.05	128.3	2.47	−56.5	−69.7
44,000	4.59	116.6	2.24	−56.5	−69.7
46,000	4.17	105.9	2.02	−56.5	−69.7
48,000	3.79	96.3	1.85	−56.5	−69.7
50,000	3.44	87.4	1.68	−56.5	−69.7
55,000	2.71	68.6	1.32	Temperature remains constant	
60,000	2.14	54.4	1.04		

Figure 9-33. *Standard atmosphere table.*

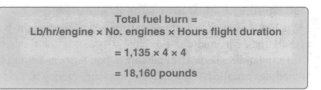

Total fuel burn =
Lb/hr/engine × No. engines × Hours flight duration

= 1,135 × 4 × 4

= 18,160 pounds

Figure 9-35. *Determining the total fuel burn for a 4-hour cruise.*

7. Draw a horizontal line to the left from the intersection of the Below Standard diagonal and the 15.3 °C temperature deviation vertical line. This line crosses the fuel flow–100 pounds per hour per engine index at 11.35 and indicates that each of the four engines burns 1,135 (100 × 11.35) pounds of fuel per hour. The total fuel burn for the 4-hour cruise is shown in *Figure 9-35*.

The airplane gross weight was 140,000 pounds at takeoff with 18,160 pounds of fuel burned during cruise and 1,350 pounds burned during the approach and landing phase. This leaves a landing weight of 140,000 − (18,160 + 1,350) = 120,490 pounds.

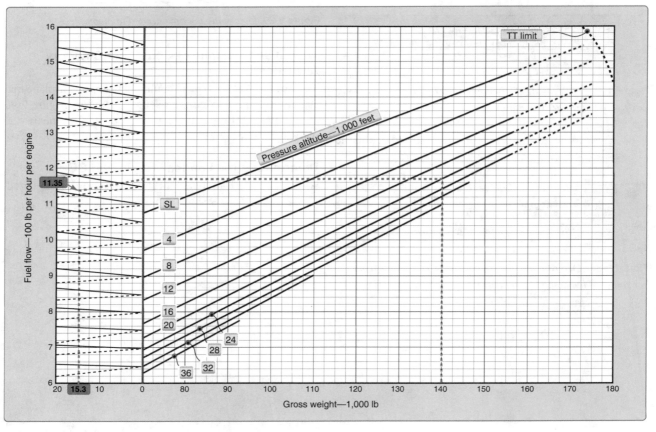

Figure 9-34. *Gross weight table.*

Determining Fuel Dump Time in Minutes

Most large aircraft are approved for a greater weight for takeoff than for landing. To make it possible for them to return to landing soon after takeoff, a fuel jettison system is sometimes installed. It is important in an emergency situation that the flight crew be able to dump enough fuel to lower the weight to its allowed landing weight. This is done by timing the dumping process.

In this example, the aircraft has two engines operating and these specifications apply:

Cruise weight...171,000 lb

Maximum landing weight..............................142,500 lb

Time from start of dump to landing..............19 minutes

Average fuel flow during:

Dumping and descent ....3,170 lb/hr/eng

Fuel dump rate ....2,300 lb/minute

To calculate the fuel dump time in minutes:

1. Determine the amount of weight the aircraft must lose to reach the maximum allowable landing weight. [Figure 9-36]

```
     171,000 lb cruise weight
   − 142,500 lb maximum landing weight
     28,500 lb required reduction
```

Figure 9-36. *Determining the amount of weight the aircraft must lose to reach the maximum allowable landing weight.*

2. Determine the amount of fuel burned from the beginning of the dump to touchdown. [Figure 9-37]

$$\text{Fuel flow} = \frac{3{,}170 \text{ lb/hr/engine}}{60}$$

$$= 52.83 \text{ lb/min engine}$$

Figure 9-37. *Determining the amount of fuel burned from the beginning of the dump to touchdown.*

For both engines, this is $52.83 \times 2 = 105.66$ lb/minute.

The engines burn 105.66 lbs of fuel per min for 19 minutes (the duration of the dump), which calculates to 2007.54 pounds of fuel burned between the beginning of the dump and touchdown.

3. Determine the amount of fuel needed to dump by subtracting the amount of fuel burned during the dump from the required weight reduction. [Figure 9-38]

```
     28,500.00 lb required weight reduction
   − 2,007.54 lb fuel burned after start of dumping
     26,492.46 lb fuel to be dumped
```

Figure 9-38. *Determining the amount of fuel needed to dump.*

4. Determine the time needed to dump this amount of fuel by dividing the number of pounds of fuel to dump by the dump rate. [Figure 9-39]

$$\frac{26{,}492.46}{2{,}300} = 11.52 \text{ minutes}$$

Figure 9-39. *Determine the time needed to dump fuel.*

Weight and Balance of Commuter Category Airplanes

The Beech 1900 is a typical commuter category airplane that can be configured to carry passengers or cargo. *Figure 9-40* shows the loading data of this type of airplane in the passenger configuration.

Determining the Loaded Weight and CG

As this airplane is prepared for flight, a manifest is prepared. [Figure 9-41]

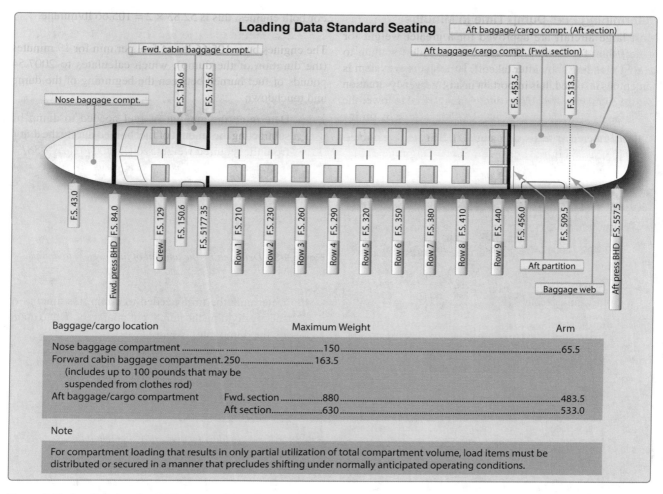

Figure 9-40. *Loading data for passenger configuration.*

Item	Weight	Arm	Moment/100	CG
Airplane basic EW	9,226		25,823	
Crew	340	129	439	
Passengers				
Row 1	300	210	600	
Row 2	250	230	575	
Row 3	190	260	494	
Row 4	170	290	493	
Row 5	190	320	608	
Row 6	340	350	1,190	
Row 7	190	380	722	
Row 8		410		
Row 9		440		
Baggage				
Nose		65.5		
Forward cabin	100	163.6	164	
Aft (forward section)	200	483.5	967	
Aft (aft section)	600	533.0	3,198	
Fuel jet A @ +25 °C				
390 gallons	2,633		7,866	
	14,729		43,139	292.9

Figure 9-41. *Determining the loaded weight and CG of a Beech 1900 in the passenger configuration.*

1. The crew weight and the weight of each passenger is entered into the manifest. The moment/100 for each occupant is determined by multiplying the weight by the arm and dividing by 100. This data is available in the AFM and is shown in the Weight and Moments—Occupants table. *[Figure 9-42]*

2. The weight of the baggage in each compartment used is entered with its moment/100. This is determined in the Weights and Moments—Baggage table. *[Figure 9-43]*

3. Determine the weight of the fuel. Jet A fuel has a nominal specific gravity at +15 °C of 0.812 and weighs 6.8 pounds per gallon, but at +25 °C, according to the Density Variation of Aviation Fuel Chart *[Figure 9-44]*, it weighs 6.75 lb/gal. Using this

Useful Load Weights and Moments—Occupants

Weight	Crew F.S. 129	Cabin seats F.S. 200	F.S. 230	F.S. 260	F.S. 290	F.S. 320	F.S. 350	F.S. 380	F.S. 410	F.S. 440
		Moment/100								
80	103	160	184	208	232	256	280	304	328	352
90	116	180	207	234	261	288	315	342	369	396
100	129	200	230	260	290	320	350	380	410	440
110	142	220	253	286	319	352	385	418	451	484
120	155	240	276	312	348	384	420	456	492	528
130	168	260	299	338	377	416	455	494	533	572
140	181	280	322	364	406	448	490	532	574	616
150	194	300	345	390	435	480	525	570	615	660
160	206	320	368	416	464	512	560	608	656	704
170	219	340	391	442	493	544	595	646	697	748
180	232	360	414	468	522	576	630	684	738	792
190	245	380	437	494	551	608	665	722	779	836
200	258	400	460	520	680	640	700	760	820	880
210	271	420	483	546	609	672	735	798	861	924
220	284	440	506	572	638	704	770	836	902	968
230	297	460	529	598	667	736	805	874	943	1012
240	310	480	552	624	696	768	840	912	984	1056
250	323	500	575	650	725	800	875	950	1025	1100

Figure 9-42. *Weight and moments—occupants.*

Useful Load Weights and Moments—Baggage

Weight	Nose baggage compartment F.S. 65.5	Forward cabin baggage compartment F.S. 163.6	AFT baggage/ cargo compartment (Forward section) F.S. 483.5	AFT baggage/ cargo compartment (Aft section) F.S. 533.0
		Moment/100		
10	7	16	48	53
20	13	33	97	107
30	20	49	145	160
40	26	65	193	213
50	33	82	242	266
60	39	98	290	320
70	46	115	338	373
80	52	131	387	426
90	59	147	435	480
100	66	164	484	533
150	98	245	725	800
200		327	967	1066
250		409	1209	1332
300			1450	1599
350			1692	1866
400			1934	2132
450			2176	2398
500			2418	2665
550			2659	2932
600			2901	3198
630			3046	3358
650			3143	
700			3384	
750			3626	
800			3868	
850			4110	
880			4255	

Figure 9-43. *Weight and moments—baggage.*

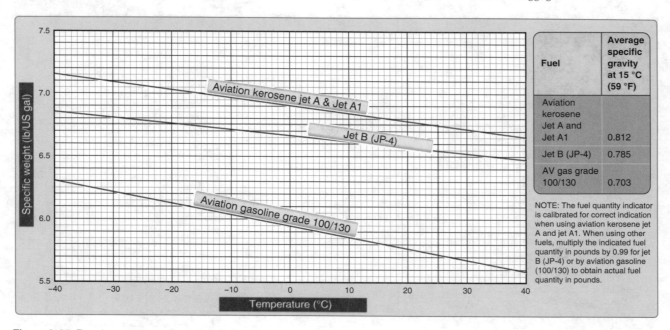

Figure 9-44. *Density variation of aviation fuel.*

Fuel	Average specific gravity at 15 °C (59 °F)
Aviation kerosene Jet A and Jet A1	0.812
Jet B (JP-4)	0.785
AV gas grade 100/130	0.703

NOTE: The fuel quantity indicator is calibrated for correct indication when using aviation kerosene jet A and jet A1. When using other fuels, multiply the indicated fuel quantity in pounds by 0.99 for jet B (JP-4) or by aviation gasoline (100/130) to obtain actual fuel quantity in pounds.

chart, determine the weights and moment/100 for 390 gallons of Jet A fuel by interpolating between those for 6.7 lb/gal and 6.8 lb/gal. The 390 gallons of fuel at this temperature weighs 2,633 pounds, and its moment index is 7,866 lb-in/100.

4. Add all of the weights and all of the moment indexes. Divide the total moment index by the total weight, and multiply this by the reduction factor of 100. The total weight is 14,729 pounds; the total moment index is 43,139 lb-in/100. The CG is located at fuselage station 292.9. [Figure 9-45]

5. Check to determine that the CG is within limits for this weight. Refer to the Weight and Balance Diagram. [Figure 9-46] Draw a horizontal line across the envelope at 14,729 pounds of weight and a vertical line from the CG of 292.9 inches aft of the datum. These lines cross inside the envelope, verifying the CG is within limits for this weight.

Useful Load Weights and Moments—Usable Fuel								
Gallons	6.5 lb/gal		6.6 lb/gal		6.7 lb/gal		6.8 lb/gal	
	Weight	Moment 100	Weight	Moment 100	Weight	Moment 100	Weight	Moment 100
10	65	197	66	200	67	203	68	206
20	130	394	132	401	134	407	136	413
30	195	592	198	601	201	610	204	619
40	260	789	264	802	268	814	272	826
50	325	987	330	1,002	335	1,018	340	1,033
60	390	1,185	396	1,203	402	1,222	408	1,240
70	455	1,383	462	1,404	469	1,426	476	1,447
80	520	1,581	528	1,605	536	1,630	544	1,654
90	585	1,779	594	1,806	603	1,834	612	1,861
100	650	1,977	660	2,007	670	2,038	680	2,068
110	715	2,175	726	2,208	737	2,242	748	2,275
120	780	2,372	792	2,409	804	2,445	816	2,482
130	845	2,569	858	2,608	871	2,648	884	2,687
140	910	2,765	924	2,808	938	2,850	952	2,893
150	975	2,962	990	3,007	1,005	3,053	1,020	3,099
160	1,040	3,157	1,056	3,205	1,072	3,254	1,088	3,303
170	1,106	3,351	1,122	3,403	1,139	3,454	1,156	3,506
180	1,170	3,545	1,188	3,600	1,206	3,654	1,224	3,709
190	1,235	3,739	1,254	3,797	1,273	3,854	1,292	3,912
200	1,300	3,932	1,320	3,992	1,340	4,053	1,360	4,113
210	1,365	4,124	1,386	4,187	1,407	4,250	1,428	4,314
220	1,430	4,315	1,452	4,382	1,474	4,448	1,496	4,514
230	1,495	4,507	1,518	4,576	1,541	4,646	1,564	4,715
240	1,560	4,698	1,584	4,770	1,608	4,843	1,632	4,915
250	1,625	4,889	1,650	4,964	1,675	5,040	1,700	5,115
260	1,690	5,080	1,716	5,158	1,742	5,236	1,768	5,315
270	1,755	5,271	1,782	5,352	1,809	5,433	1,836	5,514
280	1,820	5,462	1,848	5,546	1,876	5,630	1,904	5,714
290	1,885	5,651	1,914	5,738	1,943	5,825	1,972	5,912
300	1,950	5,842	1,980	5,932	2,010	6,022	2,040	6,112
310	2,015	6,032	2,046	6,125	2,077	6,218	2,108	6,311
320	2,080	6,225	2,112	6,321	2,144	6,416	2,176	6,512
330	2,145	6,417	1,278	6,516	2,211	6,615	2,244	6,713
340	2,210	6,610	2,244	6,711	2,278	6,813	2,312	6,915
350	2,275	6,802	2,310	6,907	2,345	7,011	2,380	7,116
360	2,340	6,995	2,376	7,103	2,412	7,210	2,448	7,318
370	2,405	7,188	2,442	7,299	2,479	7,409	2,516	7,520
380	2,470	7,381	2,508	7,495	2,546	7,609	2,584	7,722
390	2,535	7,575	2,574	7,691	2,613	7,808	2,652	7,924
400	2,600	7,768	2,640	7,888	2,680	8,007	2,720	8,127
410	2,665	7,962	2,706	8,085	2,747	8,207	2,788	8,330
420	2,730	8,156	2,772	8,282	2,814	8,407	2,856	8,532
425	2,763	8,259	2,805	8,386	2,848	8,513	2,890	8,640

Figure 9-45. *Weights and moments—usable fuel.*

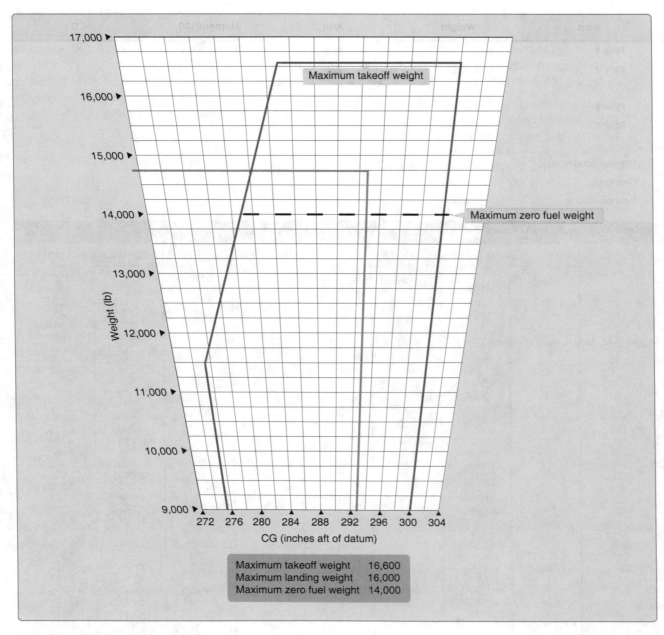

Figure 9-46. *Weight and balance diagram.*

Determining the Changes in CG When Passengers Are Shifted

Using the loaded weight and CG of the Beech 1900, calculate the change in CG when the passengers in rows 1 and 2 are moved to rows 8 and 9. *[Figure 9-47]* Note that there is no weight change, but the moment index has been increased by 1,155 pound-inches/100 to 44,294. The new CG is at fuselage station 300.7. *[Figure 9-48]*

This type of problem is usually solved by using the following two formulas. The total amount of weight shifted is 550 pounds (300 + 250) and both rows of passengers have moved aft by 210 inches (410 – 200 and 440 – 230). The CG has been shifted aft by 7.8 inches, and the new CG is at station 300.7. *[Figure 9-49]*

Item	Weight	Arm	Moment/100	CG
Row 1	(–) 300	200	(–) 600	
Row 2	(–) 250	230	(–) 575	
Row 8	(+) 300	410	(+) 1,230	
Row 9	(+) 250	440	(+) 1,100	
Original conditions	14,729		43,139	
Changes	0		(+) 1,155	
New conditions	14,729		44,294	300.7

Figure 9-47. *Changes in CG caused by shifting passenger seats.*

$$CG = \left(\frac{43,139 + 1,155}{14,729}\right) \times 100$$

$$= 300.7$$

Figure 9-48. *Determining the new CG at fuselage station.*

$$\Delta CG = \frac{\text{Weight shifted} \times \text{Distance shifted}}{\text{Total weight}}$$

$$= \frac{550 \times 210}{14,729}$$

$$= 7.8 \text{ inches}$$

$$CG = \text{Original CG} + \Delta CG$$

$$= 292.9 + 7.8$$

$$= 300.7 \text{ inches aft of datum}$$

Figure 9-49. *Determining the new CG at station after CG has shifted aft.*

In a large cabin aircraft with high-density seating such as the B737-800, the operator must account for the seating of passengers in the cabin *[Figure 9-50]*. If assigned seating is used to determine passenger location, the operator must implement procedures to ensure the assignment of passenger seating is incorporated into the loading procedure.

It is recommended that the operator take into account the possibility that some passengers may not sit in their assigned seats.

If the actual seating location of each passenger is not known, the operator may assume that all passengers are seated uniformly throughout the cabin or a specified subsection of the cabin. Reasonable assumptions can be made about the manner in which people distribute themselves throughout the cabin. For example, window seats are occupied first, followed by aisle seats, followed by the remaining seats (window-aisle-remaining seating). Both forward and rear loading conditions should be considered. The passengers may fill up the window, aisle, and remaining seats from the front of the aircraft to the back, or the back to the front.

If necessary, the operator may divide the passenger cabin into subsections or zones and manage the loading of each zone individually. It can be assumed that passengers will be sitting uniformly throughout each zone.

Another consideration is the inflight movement of passengers, crew, and equipment. It is assumed that all passengers, crew, and equipment are secured when the aircraft is in the takeoff or landing configuration. Standard operating procedures

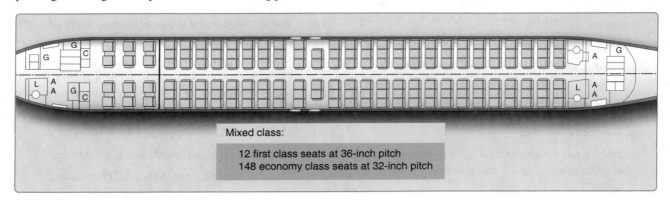

Mixed class:

12 first class seats at 36-inch pitch
148 economy class seats at 32-inch pitch

Figure 9-50. *One passenger configuration of a B737-800.*

should be taken into account. Examples of items that can move during flight are:

- Flight deck crew members moving to the lavatory.
- Flight attendants moving throughout the cabin.
- Service carts moving throughout the cabin.
- Passengers moving throughout the cabin.
- Passengers moving to the lavatory.

Determining Changes in Weight and CG When the Aircraft Is Operated in Its Cargo Configuration

To determine changes in weight and CG when the aircraft is operated in its cargo configuration, the Beech 1900 is used as an example. *Figure 9-51* illustrates the airplane configuration. Notice that the arm of each cargo section is the centroid of that section.

The flight manifest of the Beech 1900 in the cargo configuration is illustrated in *Figure 9-52*. The BOW includes the pilots and their baggage and there is no separate item for them.

At the standard temperature of 15 °C, the fuel weighs 6.8 pounds per gallon. Refer to *Figure 9-45* to determine the weight and moment index of 370 gallons of Jet A fuel. The CG under these loading conditions is located at station 296.2.

Determining the CG Shift When Cargo Is Moved From One Section to Another

To calculate the CG when cargo is shifted from one section to another, use the formula found in *Figure 9-53*. If the cargo is moved forward, the CG is subtracted from the original CG. If the cargo is shifted aft, add the CG to the original.

Determining the CG Shift When Cargo Is Added or Removed

To calculate the CG when cargo is added or removed, add or subtract the weight and moment index of the affected cargo to the original loading chart. Determine the new CG by dividing the new moment index by the new total weight, and multiply this by the reduction factor. [*Figure 9-54*]

Determining Which Limits Are Exceeded

When preparing an aircraft for flight, consider all parameters and check to determine that no limits have been exceeded. Consider the parameters below, and determine which limit, if any, has been exceeded.

- The aircraft in this example has a basic empty weight of 9,005 pounds and a moment index of 25,934 pound inches/100.

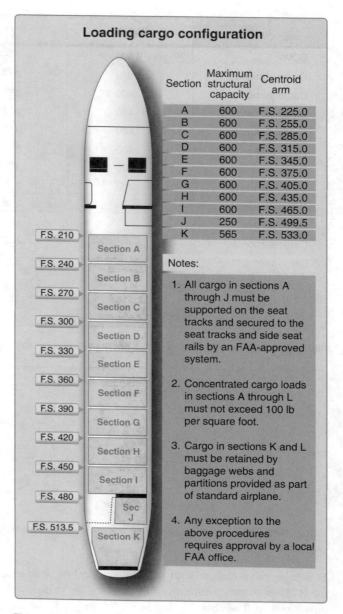

Figure 9-51. *Loading data for cargo configuration.*

- The crew weight is 340 pounds and its moment/100 is 439.
- The passengers and baggage have a weight of 3,950 pounds and a moment/100 of 13,221.
- The fuel is computed at 6.8 lb/gal. The ramp load is 340 gallons or 2,312 pounds. Fuel used for start and taxi is 20 gallons, or 136 pounds. Fuel remaining at landing is 100 gallons, or 680 pounds.
- Maximum takeoff weight is 16,600 pounds.
- Maximum zero fuel weight is 14,000 pounds.
- Maximum landing weight is 16,000 pounds.

Item	Weight	Arm	Moment/100	CG
BOW	9,005		25,934	
Cargo section A	300	225.0	675	
Cargo section B	400	255.0	1,020	
Cargo section C	450	285.0	1,283	
Cargo section D	600	315.0	1,890	
Cargo section E	600	345.0	2,070	
Cargo section F	600	375.0	2,250	
Cargo section G	200	405.0	810	
Cargo section H		435.0		
Cargo section I		465.0		
Cargo section J		499.5		
Cargo section K		533.0		
Fuel jet A at +15 °C				
gallons 370	2,516		7,520	
	14,671		43,452	296.2

Figure 9-52. *Flight manifest of a Beech 1900 in the cargo configuration.*

$$\Delta CG = \frac{\text{Weight shifted x Distance shifted}}{\text{Total weight}}$$

Figure 9-53. *Shifting cargo from one section to another.*

$$CG = \frac{\text{Total moment index}}{\text{Total weight}} \times \text{Reduction factor}$$

Figure 9-54. *Determining the new CG by dividing the new moment index by the new total weight, multiplied by the reduction factor.*

Take these steps to determine which limit, if any, is exceeded:

1. Determine the zero fuel weight, which is the weight of the aircraft with all of the useful load except the fuel onboard. *[Figure 9-55]*

Item	Weight (lb)	Moment	CG
Basic empty weight	9,005	25,934	
Crew	340	439	
Passengers & baggage	3,950	13,221	
Zero fuel weight	13,295	39,594	

Figure 9-55. *Determining the zero fuel weight.*

The zero fuel weight of 13,295 pounds is less than the maximum of 14,000 pounds, so this parameter is acceptable.

2. Determine the takeoff weight and CG. The takeoff weight is the zero fuel weight plus the weight of the ramp load of fuel, minus the weight of the fuel used for start and taxi. The takeoff CG is the moment/100 divided by the weight, and then the result multiplied by 100. The takeoff weight of 15,471 pounds is below the maximum takeoff weight of 16,600 pounds, and a check of the weight and balance diagram shows that the CG at station 298.0 is also within limits. *[Figure 9-56]*

Item	Weight (lb)	Moment	CG
Zero fuel weight	13,295	39,594	
Takeoff fuel 320 gal			
Ramp load–fuel for start & taxi			
340 – 20 = 320 gal	2,176	6,512	
Takeoff weight	15,471	46,106	298.0

Figure 9-56. *Determining the takeoff weight and CG.*

3. Determine the landing weight and CG. This is the zero fuel weight plus the weight of fuel at landing. *[Figure 9-57]*

Item	Weight (lb)	Moment	CG
Zero fuel weight	13,295	39,594	
Fuel at landing 100 gal	680	1,977	
Landing weight	13,975	41,571	297.5

Figure 9-57. *Determining the landing weight and CG.*

The landing weight of 13,975 pounds is less than the maximum landing weight of 14,000 to 16,000 pounds. According to the weight and balance diagram, the landing CG at station 297.5 is also within limits.

Chapter 10
Use of Computer for Weight and Balance Computations

Introduction

Almost all weight and balance problems involve only simple math. This allows slide rules and hand-held electronic calculators to relieve much of the tedium involved with these problems. This chapter compares the methods of determining the center of gravity (CG) of an airplane while it is being weighed. First, it shows how to determine the CG using a simple electronic calculator, then solves the same problem using an E6-B flight computer. Finally, it shows how to solve it using a dedicated electronic flight computer.

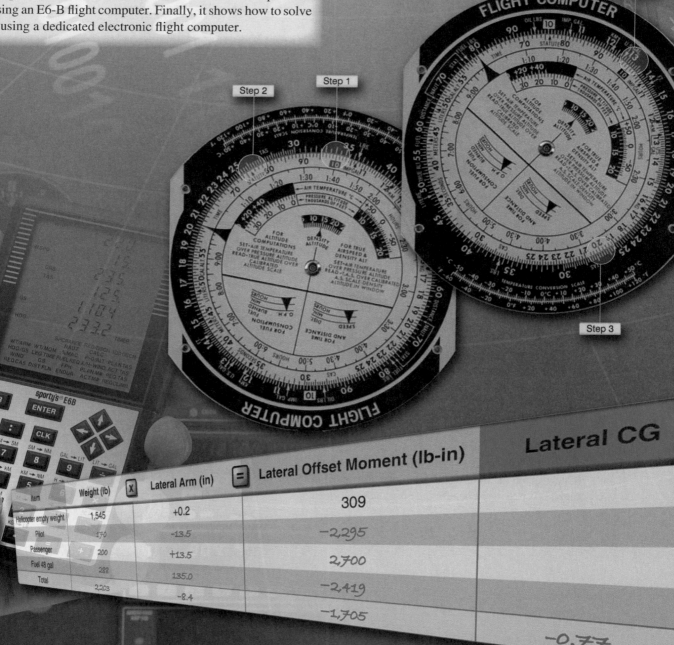

Step 4

Step 1

Step 2

Step 3

Lateral CG

Item	Weight (lb)	X	Lateral Arm (in)	=	Lateral Offset Moment (lb-in)
Helicopter empty weight	1,545		+0.2		309
Pilot	170		-13.5		-2,295
Passenger	200		+13.5		2,700
Fuel 48 gal	288		135.0		-2,419
Total	2,203		-8.4		-1,705
					-0.77

Examples of typical weight and balance problems (solved with an electronic calculator) that pilots and airframe and powerplant (A&P) maintenance technicians encounter throughout their aviation endeavors are shown later in this chapter.

Electronic Calculator

Determining the CG of an airplane in inches for the main-wheel weighing points can be done with any simple electronic calculator that has addition (+), subtraction (−), multiplication (×), and division (÷) functions. *[Figure 10-1]* Scientific calculators with such additional functions as memory (M), parentheses (( )), plus or minus (+/−), exponential (y^x), reciprocal (1/x), and percentage (%) functions allow more complex problems to be solved or simple problems to be solved using fewer steps.

Figure 10-1. *A typical electronic calculator is useful for solving most types of weight and balance problems.*

According to *Figure 10-2*, the weight of the nosewheel (F) is 340 pounds, the distance between main wheels and nosewheel (L) is −78 inches, and the total weight (W) of the airplane is 2,006 pounds. L is negative because the nosewheel is ahead of the main wheels.

Weighing Point	Weight (lb)	Arm (in)
Right side	830	0
Left side	836	0
Nose	340	−78
Total	2,006	

Figure 10-2. *Weight and balance data of a typical nosewheel airplane.*

To determine the CG, use this formula:

$$CG = \frac{F \times L}{W}$$

$$= \frac{340 \times -78}{2,006}$$

Key the data into the calculator and press the equal (=) key. The answer should read as follows:

(340)(×)(78)(+/−)(÷)(2006)(=) −13.2

The arm of the nosewheel is negative, so the CG is −13.2 or 13.2 inches ahead of the main wheel weighing points.

E6-B Flight Computer

The E6-B uses a special kind of slide rule. Instead of its scales going from 1 to 10, as on a normal slide rule, both scales go from 10 to 100. The E6-B cannot be used for addition or subtraction, but it is useful for making calculations involving multiplication and division. Its accuracy is limited, but it is sufficiently accurate for most weight and balance problems.

The same problem that was just solved with the electronic calculator can be solved on an E6-B by following these steps:

$$CG = \frac{F \times L}{W}$$

$$= \frac{340 \times -78}{2,006}$$

First, multiply 340 by 78 (disregard the minus sign) *[Figure 10-3]*:

- Step 1—place 10 on the inner scale (this is the index opposite 34 on the outer scale that represents 340).

- Step 2—opposite 78 on the inner scale, read 26.5 on the outer scale.

  Determine the value of these digits by estimating: $300 \times 80 = 24,000$, so $340 \times 78 = 26,500$.

  Then, divide 26,500 by 2,006 *[Figure 10-4]*:

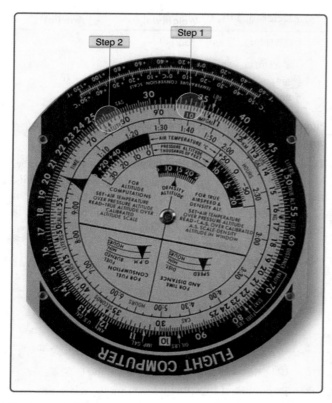

Figure 10-3. *E6-B computer set up to multiply 340 by 78.*

Figure 10-4. *E6-B computer set up to divide 26,500 by 2,006.*

- Step 3—on the inner scale, place 20, which represents 2,006 opposite 26.5 on the outer scale (26.5 represents 26,500).

- Step 4—opposite the index, 10, on the inner scale read 13.2 on the outer scale.

  Determine the value of 13.2 by estimating: 20,000 ÷ 2000 = 10, so 26,500 ÷ 2,006 = 13.2.

  The arm (–78) is negative, so the CG is also negative.

The CG is –13.2 inches or 13.2 inches ahead of the datum.

Dedicated Electronic Flight Computer

Dedicated electronic flight computers, like the one in *Figure 10-5,* are programmed to solve many flight problems such as wind correction, heading and ground speed, endurance, and true airspeed (TAS), as well as weight and balance problems.

Figure 10-5. *Dedicated electronic flight computers are programmed to solve weight and balance problems, as well as flight problems.*

The problem just solved with an electronic calculator and an E6-B can also be solved with a dedicated flight computer using the information shown in *Figure 10-2.* Each flight computer handles the problems in a slightly different way, but all are programmed with prompts that solicit the required data to be inputted so there is no need to memorize any formulas. Weight and arms are inputted as called for, and a running total of the weight, moment, and CG are displayed.

Typical Weight and Balance Problems

A hand-held electronic calculator like the one in *Figure 10-5* is a valuable tool for solving weight and balance problems. It can be used for a variety of problems and has a high degree of accuracy. The examples given here are solved with a calculator using only the $(\times),(\div),(+),(-)$, and $(+/-)$ functions. If other functions are available on your calculator, some of the steps may be simplified.

Determining CG in Inches From the Datum

This type of problem is solved by first determining the location of the CG in inches from the main wheel weighing points, then measuring this location in inches from the datum. There are four types of problems involving the location of the CG relative to the datum.

Nosewheel Airplane With Datum Ahead of the Main Wheels

The datum (D) is 128 inches ahead of the main wheel weighing points; the weight of the nosewheel (F) is 340 pounds, and the distance between main wheels and nosewheel (L) is 78 inches. The total weight (W) of the airplane is 2,006 pounds. Refer to *Figure 3-5* on page 3-5.

Use this formula:

$$CG = D - \left(\frac{F \times L}{W} \right)$$

1. Determine the CG in inches from the main wheel:
   $(340)(\times)(78)(\div)(2006)(=)\ 13.2$

2. Determine the CG in inches form the datum:
   $(128)(-)(13.2)(=)\ 114.8$

   The CG is 114.8 inches behind the datum.

Nosewheel Airplane With Datum Behind the Main Wheels

The datum (D) is 75 inches behind the main wheel weighing points, the weight of the nosewheel (F) is 340 pounds, and the distance between main wheels and nosewheel (L) is 78 inches. The total weight (W) of the airplane is 2,006 pounds. Refer to *Figure 3-6* on page 3-5.

Use this formula:

$$CG = - \left(D + \frac{F \times L}{W} \right)$$

1. Determine the CG in inches from the main wheels:
   $(340)(\times)(78)(\div)(2006)(=)\ 13.2$

2. Determine the CG in inches from the datum:
   $(75)(+)(13.2)(=)\ 88.2$

   The minus sign before the parenthesis in the formula means the answer is negative. The CG is 88.2 inches ahead of the datum (-88.2).

Tailwheel Airplane With Datum Ahead of the Main Wheels

The datum (D) is 7.5 inches ahead of the main wheel weighing points, the weight of the tailwheel (R) is 67 pounds, and the distance between main wheels and tailwheel (L) is 222 inches. The total weight (W) of the airplane is 1,218 pounds. Refer to *Figure 3-7* on page 3-6.

Use this formula:

$$CG = \left(D + \frac{R \times L}{W} \right)$$

1. Determine the CG in inches from the main wheels.
   $(67)(\times)(222)(\div)(1218)(=)\ 12.2$

2. Determine the CG in inches from the datum:
   $(7.5)(+)(12.2)(=)\ 19.7$

   The CG is 19.7 inches behind the datum.

Tailwheel Airplane With Datum Behind the Main Wheels

The datum (D) is 80 inches behind the main wheel weighing points, the weight of the tailwheel (R) is 67 pounds, and the distance between main wheels and tailwheel (L) is 222 inches. The total weight (W) of the airplane is 1,218 pounds. Refer to *Figure 3-8* on page 3-6.

Use this formula:

$$CG = -D + \left(\frac{R \times L}{W} \right)$$

1. Determine the CG in inches from the main wheels:
   $(67)(\times)(222)(\div)(1218)(=)\ 12.2$

2. Determine the CG in inches from the datum:
   $(80)(+/-)(+)(12.2)(=)\ -67.8$

   The CG is 67.8 inches ahead of the datum.

Weight Point	Weight (lb)	Arm (in)	Moment (lb-in)	CG
Right side	830	128	106,240	
Left side	836	128	107,008	
Nose	340	50	17,000	
Total	2,006		230,248	114.8

Figure 10-6. *Specifications for determining the CG of an airplane using weight and arm.*

Determining CG, Given Weights, and Arms

Some weight and balance problems involve weights and arms to determine the moments. Divide the total moment by the total weight to determine the CG. *Figure 10-6* contains the specifications for determining the CG using weights and arms.

Determine the CG by using the data in *Figure 10-6* and following these steps:

1. Determine the total weight and record this number:

    (830)(+)(836)(+)(340)(=) 2,006

2. Determine the moment of each weighing point and record them:

    (830)(×)(128)(=) 106,240

    (836)(×)(128)(=) 107,008

    (340)(×)(50)(=) 17,000

3. Determine the total moment and divide this by the total weight:

    (106240)(+)(107008)(+)(17000)(=)(÷)(2006)(=) 114.8

This airplane weighs 2,006 pounds and its CG is 114.8 inches from the datum.

Determining CG, Given Weights, and Moment Indexes

Other weight and balance problems involve weights and moment indexes, such as moment/100 or moment/1,000. To determine the CG, add all the weights and all the moment indexes. Then, divide the total moment index by the total weight and multiply the answer by the reduction factor. *Figure 10-7* contains the specifications for determining the

Weighing Point	Weight (lb)	Moment/100	CG
Right side	830	1,062.4	
Left side	836	1,070.1	
Nose	340	170	
Total	2,006	2,302.5	114.8

Figure 10-7. *Specifications for determining the CG of an airplane using weights and moment indexes.*

CG using weights and moments indexes.

Determine the CG by using the data in *Figure 10-7* and following these steps:

1. Determine the total weight and record this number:

    (830)(+)(836)(+)(340)(=) 2,006

2. Determine the total moment index, divide this by the total weight, and multiply it by the reduction factor of 100:

    (1062.4)(+)(1070.1)(+)(170)(=)(2302.5)(÷)(2006)(=)
    (1.148)(×)(100)(=) 114.8

This airplane weighs 2,006 pounds and its CG is 114.8 inches from the datum.

Determining CG in Percent Mean Aerodynamic Chord (MAC)

- The loaded CG is 42.47 inches aft of the datum.

- MAC is 61.6 inches long.

- LEMAC is at station 20.1.

1. Determine the distance between the CG and LEMAC:

    (42.47)(−)(20.1)(=) 22.37

2. Then, use this formula:

    (22.37)(×)(100)(÷)(61.6)(=) 36.3

The CG of this airplane is located at 36.3 percent MAC.

Determining Lateral CG of a Helicopter

For a helicopter, it is often necessary to determine not only the longitudinal CG, but the lateral CG as well. Lateral CG is measured from butt line zero (BL 0). All items and moments to the left of BL 0 are negative, and all those to the right of BL 0 are positive. *Figure 10-8* contains the specifications for determining the lateral CG of a typical helicopter.

Determine the lateral CG by using the data in *Figure 10-8* and following these steps:

1. Add all of the weights:

   (1545)(+)(170)(+)(200)(+)(288)(=) 2,203

2. Multiply the lateral arm (the distance between butt line zero and the CG of each item) by its weight to get the lateral offset moment of each item. Moments to the right of BL 0 are positive and those to the left are negative.

   (1,545)(×)(.2)(=) 309

   (170)(×)(13.5)(+/−)(=) −2,295

   (200)(×)(13.5)(=) 2,700

   (288)(×)(8.4)(+/−)(=) −2,419

3. Determine the algebraic sum of the lateral offset moments.

   (309)(+)(2295)(+/−)(+)(2700)(+)(2419)(+/−)(=) −1,705

4. Divide the sum of the moments by the total weight to determine the lateral CG.

   (1705)(+/−)(÷)(2203)(=) −0.77

The lateral CG is 0.77 inch to the left of BL0.

Determining ΔCG Caused by Shifting Weights

Fifty pounds of baggage is shifted from the aft baggage compartment at station 246 to the forward compartment at station 118. The total airplane weight is 4,709 pounds. How much does the CG shift?

1. Determine the number of inches the baggage is shifted:

   (246)(−)(118)(=) 128

2. Use this formula:

$$\Delta CG = \frac{\text{Weight shifted} \times \text{Distance weight is shifted}}{\text{Total weight}}$$

   (50)(×)(128)(÷)(4709)(=) 1.36

The CG is shifted forward 1.36 inches.

Determining Weight Shifted to Cause Specified ΔCG

How much weight must be shifted from the aft baggage compartment at station 246 to the forward compartment at station 118 to move the CG forward 2 inches? The total weight of the airplane is 4,709 pounds.

1. Determine the number of inches the baggage is shifted:

$$\text{Weight shifted} = \frac{\text{Total weight shifted} \times \Delta CG}{\text{Distance weight is shifted}}$$

   (246)(−)(118)(=) 128

2. Use this formula:

   (2)(×)(4709)(÷)(128)(=) 73.6

Moving 73.6 pounds of baggage from the aft compartment to forward compartment shifts the CG forward 2 inches.

Determining Distance Weight Is Shifted to Move CG a Specific Distance

How many inches aft does a 56 pound battery need to be moved to shift the CG aft by 1.5 inches? The total weight of the airplane is 4,026 pounds.

Use this formula:

$$\text{Distance weight is shifted} = \frac{\text{Total weight} \times \Delta CG}{\text{Weight shifted}}$$

(1.5)(×)(4026)(÷)(56)(=) 107.8

Moving the battery aft by 107.8 inches shifts the CG aft 1.5 inches.

Item	Weight (lb)	X	Lateral Arm (in)	=	Lateral Offset Moment (lb-in)	Lateral CG
Helicopter empty weight	1,545		+0.2		309	
Pilot	170		−13.5		−2,295	
Passenger	200		+13.5		2,700	
Fuel (48 gal)	288		135.0		−2,419	
Total	2,203		−8.4		−1,705	−0.77

Figure 10-8. *Specifications for determining the lateral CG of a helicopter.*

Determining Total Weight of an Aircraft With a Specified ΔCG When Cargo Is Moved

What is the total weight of an airplane if moving 500 pounds of cargo 96 inches forward shifts the CG 2.0 inches?

Use this formula:

$$\text{Total weight} = \frac{\text{Weight shifted} \times \text{Distance weight is shifted}}{\Delta\,CG}$$

(500)(×)(96)(÷)(2)(=) 24,000

Moving 500 pounds of cargo 96 inches forward causes a 2.0-inch shift in CG of a 24,000-pound airplane.

Determining Amount of Ballast Needed to Move CG to a Desired Location

How much ballast must be mounted at station 228 to move the CG to its forward limit of +33? The airplane weighs 1,876 pounds and the CG is at +32.2, a distance of 0.8 inch out of limit.

Use this formula:

$$\text{Ballast weight} = \frac{\text{Aircraft empty weight} \times \text{Dist. out of limits}}{\text{Distance ballast to desired CG}}$$

(1876)(×)(.8)(÷)(195)(=) 7.7

Attaching 7.7 pounds of ballast to the bulkhead at station 228 moves the CG to +33.0.

Appendix A

Supplemental Study Materials for Aircraft Weight and Balance

FAA Publications

(check for most current revision)

- Advisory Circular (AC) 20-161, Aircraft Onboard Weight and Balance Systems
- AC 23-21, Airworthiness Compliance Checklists Used to Substantiate Major Alterations for Small Airplanes
- AC 43.13-1, Acceptable Methods, Techniques, and Practices—Aircraft Inspection and Repair
- AC 90-89, Amateur-Built Aircraft and Ultralight Flight Testing Handbook
- AC 120-27, Aircraft Weight and Balance Control
- FAA-H-8083-30, Aviation Maintenance Technician Handbook—General
- Order 8130.2, Airworthiness Certification of Aircraft and Related Products
- www.faa.gov, Light Sport Aircraft (multiple electronic documents)

Appendix B

Key Weight and Balance Locations on an Aircraft

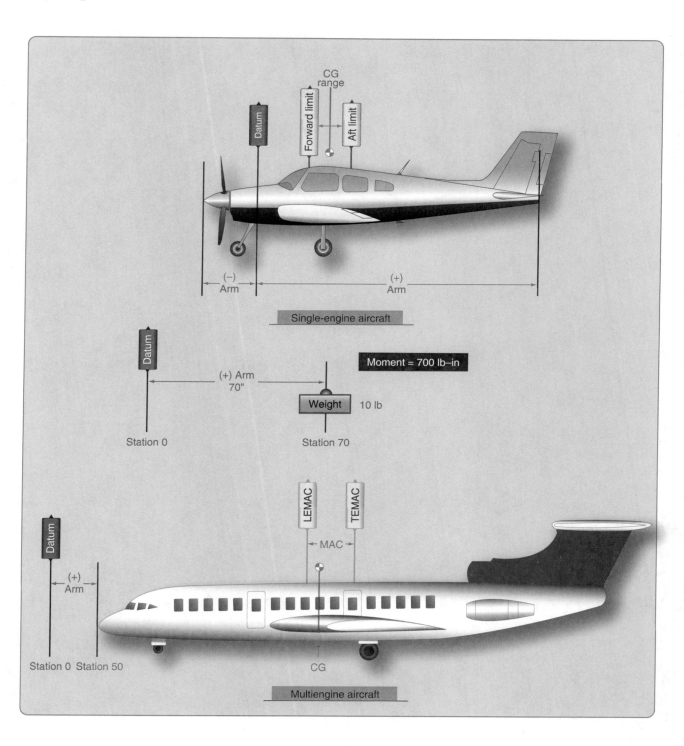

CG range

Forward limit

Aft limit

Datum

(−) Arm

(+) Arm

Single-engine aircraft

Datum

(+) Arm 70"

Moment = 700 lb–in

Weight   10 lb

Station 0

Station 70

LEMAC

TEMAC

← MAC →

Datum

(+) Arm

Station 0 Station 50

CG

Multiengine aircraft

Glossary

A note on glossary terms: over the years there has been a proliferation of aircraft weight and balance terms. This is the result of many factors, such as the Federal Aviation Administration (FAA) certification regulation under which an aircraft was constructed; the FAA regulation under which the aircraft is being operated; manufacturer standardization agreements or a combination of these and others. Examples of such terms are empty weight, licensed empty weight, basic empty weight, operational empty weight, etc.

Many of these terms may have similar meanings or sound similar. Pilots and aircraft mechanics must ensure they understand the terminology and are applying the correct values based on the procedure and situation dictating the calculations undertaken.

Occasionally, the acronym "GAMA" follows the glossary term. This indicates that it is part of the standardized format adopted by the General Aviation Manufacturers Association in 1976, known as GAMA Specification No.1. These aircraft are usually manufactured under Title 14 of the Code of Federal Regulations (14 CFR) part 23 and differ from aircraft manufactured under the earlier certification rule Civil Air Regulation (CAR) part 3 for weight and balance purposes in the condition under which empty weight was established.

Aircraft certified under 14 CFR parts 23, 25, 27, and 29 establish their certificated empty weight as required in the appropriate section of these regulations, which states that the empty weight and corresponding center of gravity (CG) must be determined by weighting the aircraft with:

- Fixed ballast
- Unusable fuel
- Full operating fluid, including oil, hydraulic fluid, and other fluids required for normal operation of the aircraft systems, except potable water, lavatory precharge water, and water intended for injection in the engine(s).

In contrast, aircraft certified under the older CARs established certificated empty weight under similar conditions as the newer aircraft, with the important exception that the aircraft weight did not include full oil, only undrainable oil. Mechanics and repair stations should consult the appropriate certification rule when reestablishing empty weight.

14 CFR part 121. The Federal regulations governing domestic, flag, and supplemental operations.

14 CFR part 135. The Federal regulations governing commuter and on-demand operations.

Adverse loaded CG check. A weight and balance check to determine that no condition of legal loading of an aircraft can move the CG outside of its allowable limits.

Aircraft specifications. Documentation containing the pertinent specifications for aircraft certificated under the CARs.

Airplane Flight manual (AFM). An FAA-approved document, prepared by the holder of a type certificate for an aircraft, that specifies the operating limitations and contains the required markings and placards and other information applicable to the regulations under which the aircraft was certificated.

Approved type certificate. A certificate of approval issued by the FAA for the design of an aircraft, engine, or propeller.

Arm. (GAMA) The horizontal distance from the reference datum to the CG of an item. The algebraic sign is plus (+) if measured aft of the datum or to the right side of the center line when considering a lateral calculation. The algebraic sign is minus (–) if measured forward of the datum or the left side of the center line when considering a lateral calculation.

Balanced laterally. Being balanced in such a way that the aircraft wings tend to remain level.

Ballast. A weight installed or carried in an aircraft to move the center of gravity to a location within its allowable limits.

Permanent ballast (fixed ballast). A weight permanently installed in an aircraft to bring its CG into allowable limits. Permanent ballast is part of the aircraft empty weight.

Temporary ballast. Weights that can be carried in a cargo compartment of an aircraft to move the location of CG for a specific flight condition. Temporary ballast must be removed when the aircraft is weighed.

Basic empty weight. (GAMA) Standard empty weight plus optional equipment.

Basic operating index. The moment of the airplane at its basic operating weight divided by the appropriate reduction factor.

Basic operating weight (BOW). The empty weight of the aircraft plus the weight of the required crew, their baggage, and other standard items, such as meals and potable water.

Bilge area. The lowest part of an aircraft structure in which water and contaminants collect.

Butt (or buttock) line zero. A line through the symmetrical center of an aircraft from nose to tail. It serves as the datum for measuring the arms used to determine the lateral CG. Lateral moments that cause the aircraft to rotate clockwise are positive (+), and those that cause it to rotate counterclockwise are negative (−).

Calendar month. A time period used by the FAA for certification and currency purposes. A calendar month extends from a given day until midnight of the last day of that month.

Civil Air Regulations (CAR). The predecessor to the Federal Aviation Regulations.

CAM. The acronym for the manuals containing the certification rules under the Civil Air Regulations.

Center of gravity (CG). (GAMA) The point at which an airplane would balance if suspended. Its distance from the reference datum is determined by dividing the total moment by the total weight of the airplane. It is the mass center of the aircraft, or the theoretical point at which the entire weight of the aircraft is assumed to be concentrated. It may be expressed in percent of MAC (mean aerodynamic cord) or in inches from the reference datum.

Center of lift. The location along the chord line of an airfoil at which all the lift forces produced by the airfoil are considered to be concentrated.

Centroid. The distance in inches aft of the datum of the center of a compartment or a fuel tank for weight and balance purposes.

CG arm. (GAMA) The arm obtained by adding the airplane's individual moments and dividing the sum by the total weight.

CG limits. (GAMA) The extreme CG locations within which the aircraft must be operated at a given weight. These limits are indicated on pertinent FAA aircraft type certificate data sheets, specifications, or weight and balance records.

CG limits envelope. An enclosed area on a graph of the airplane loaded weight and the CG location. If lines drawn from the weight and CG cross within this envelope, the airplane is properly loaded.

CG moment envelope. An enclosed area on a graph of the airplane loaded weight and loaded moment. If lines drawn from the weight and loaded moment cross within this envelope, the airplane is properly loaded.

Chord. A straight line distance across a wing from leading edge to trailing edge.

Curtailment. An operator created and FAA-approved operational loading envelope that is more restrictive than the manufacturer's CG envelope. It ensures that the aircraft will be operated within limits during all phases of flight. Curtailment typically accounts for, but is not limited to, in-flight movement of passengers and crew, service equipment, cargo variation, seating variation, etc.

Datum. An imaginary vertical plane or line from which all measurements of arms are taken. The datum is established by the manufacturer. Once the datum has been selected, all moment arms and the location of CG range are measured from this point.

Delta (Δ). The Greek symbol "Δ" means a change in something. ΔCG means a change in the center of gravity location.

Dynamic load. The actual weight of the aircraft multiplied by the load factor, or the increase in weight caused by acceleration.

Empty weight. The weight of the airframe, engines, all permanently installed equipment, and unusable fuel. Depending upon the part of the federal regulations under which the aircraft was certificated, either the undrainable oil or full reservoir of oil is included.

Empty weight center of gravity (EWCG). This is the center of gravity of the aircraft in the empty condition, containing only the items specified in the aircraft empty weight. This CG is an essential part of the weight and balance record of the aircraft.

Empty weight center of gravity range. The distance between the allowable forward and aft empty-weight CG limits.

Equipment list. A list of items approved by the FAA for installation in a particular aircraft. The list includes the name, part number, weight, and arm of the component. Installation or removal of an item in the equipment list is considered to be a minor alteration.

Fleet weight. An average weight accepted by the FAA for aircraft of identical make and model that have the same equipment installed. When a fleet weight control program is in effect, the fleet weight of the aircraft can be used rather than requiring every individual aircraft to be weighed.

Fuel jettison system. A fuel subsystem that allows the flight crew to dump fuel in an emergency to lower the weight of an aircraft to the maximum landing weight if a return to landing is required before sufficient fuel is burned off. This system must allow enough fuel to be jettisoned that the aircraft can still meet the climb requirements specified in 14 CFR part 25.

Fulcrum. The point about which a lever balances.

Index point. A location specified by the aircraft manufacturer from which arms used in weight and balance computations are measured. Arms measured from the index point are called index arms.

Interpolate. Determine a value in a range between two known values.

Landing weight. The takeoff weight of an aircraft minus the fuel burned and/or dumped en route.

Large aircraft (14 CFR part 1). An aircraft of more than 12,500 pounds maximum certificated takeoff weight.

Lateral balance. The balance around the roll, or longitudinal, axis.

Lateral offset moment. The moment, in pound inches, of a force that tends to rotate a helicopter about its longitudinal axis. The lateral offset moment is the product of the weight of the object and its distance from butt line zero. Lateral offset moments that tend to rotate the aircraft clockwise are positive, and those that tend to rotate it counterclockwise are negative.

LEMAC. Leading edge of the mean aerodynamic chord. A reference point for measurements, and specified in inches from the datum to allow computations to relate percent MAC to the datum.

Load cell. A component in an electronic weighing system that is placed between the jack and the jack pad on the aircraft. The load cell contains strain gauges whose resistance changes with the weight on the cell.

Load factor. The ratio of the maximum load an aircraft can sustain to the total weight of the aircraft. Normal category aircraft must have a load factor of a least 3.8; utility category aircraft, 4.4; and acrobatic category aircraft, 6.0.

Loading graph. A graph of load weight and load moment indexes. Diagonal lines for each item relate the weight to the moment index, eliminating the need for calculations.

Loading schedule. A method of calculating and documenting aircraft weight and balance prior to taxiing to ensure the aircraft will remain within all required weight and balance limitations throughout the flight.

Longitudinal axis. An imaginary line through an aircraft from nose to tail, passing through its center of gravity.

Longitudinal balance. The balance around the pitch, or lateral, axis.

MAC. Mean aerodynamic chord.

Major alteration. An alteration not listed in the aircraft, aircraft engine, or propeller specifications (1) that might appreciably affect weight, balance, structural strength, performance, powerplant operation, flight characteristics, or other qualities affecting airworthiness; or (2) that is not done according to accepted practices or cannot be done by elementary operations.

Maximum landing weight. (GAMA) The maximum weight approved for the landing touchdown.

Maximum permissible hoist load. The maximum external load that is permitted for a helicopter to carry. This load is specified in the POH.

Maximum ramp weight. (GAMA) The maximum weight approved for ground maneuver. It includes weight of start, taxi, and runup fuel.

Maximum takeoff weight. (GAMA) The maximum weight approved for the start of the takeoff run.

Maximum taxi weight. The maximum weight approved for ground maneuvers. This is the same as maximum ramp weight.

Maximum weight. The maximum authorized weight of the aircraft and all of its equipment as specified in the Type Certificate Data Sheets (TCDS) for the aircraft.

Maximum zero fuel weight. The maximum authorized weight of an aircraft without fuel. This is the total weight for a particular flight minus the fuel. It includes the aircraft and everything that is carried on the flight except the weight of the fuel.

Mean aerodynamic chord (MAC). The average distance from the leading edge to the trailing edge of the wing.

METO horsepower (maximum except takeoff HP). The maximum power allowed to be produced continuously by an engine. Takeoff power is usually limited to a given amount of time, such as 1 minute or 5 minutes.

Minimum fuel. The amount of fuel necessary for one-half hour of operation at the rated maximum-continuous power setting of the engine, which, for weight and balance purposes, is 1/12 gallon per maximum-except-takeoff (METO) horsepower. It is the maximum amount of fuel that could be used in weight and balance computations when low fuel might adversely affect the most critical balance conditions. To determine the weight of the minimum fuel in pounds, divide the METO horsepower by two.

Minor alteration. An alteration other than a major alteration. This includes alterations that are listed in the aircraft, aircraft engine, or propeller specifications.

Moment. A force that causes or tends to cause an object to rotate. It is indicated by the product of the weight of an item multiplied by its arm.

Moment. (GAMA) The product of the weight of an item multiplied by its arm. (Moment divided by a constant is used to simplify balance calculations by reducing the number of digits; see reduction factor.)

Moment index. The moment (weight times arm) divided by a reduction factor.

Moment limits versus weight envelope. An enclosed area on a graph of three parameters. The diagonal line, representing the moment/100, crosses the horizontal line, representing the weight at the vertical line, representing the CG location in inches aft of the datum. If the lines cross inside the envelope, the aircraft is loaded within its weight and CG limits.

Net weight. The weight of the aircraft minus the weight of chocks or other devices used to hold the aircraft on the scales.

Normal category. A category of aircraft certificated under 14 CFR part 23 and CAR part 3 that allows the maximum weight and CG range while restricting the maneuvers that are permitted.

PAX. The abbreviation of passengers.

Payload. (GAMA) The weight of occupants, cargo, and baggage.

Percent MAC. The distance in inches of the CG from LEMAC divided by the MAC. It is a good standard for CG location in airplanes because it permits a standard weight and balance program for different types of airplanes.

Pilot's operating handbook (POH). An FAA-approved document published by the airframe manufacturer that lists the operating conditions for a particular model of aircraft and its engine(s).

Potable water. The water carried in an aircraft for the purpose of drinking.

Ramp weight. The zero fuel weight plus all of the usable fuel on board.

Reference datum. (GAMA) An imaginary vertical plane from which all horizontal distances are measured for balance purposes.

Reduction factor. A number, usually 100 or 1,000, by which a moment is divided to produce a smaller number that is less likely to cause mathematical errors when computing the center of gravity.

Residual fuel. The fuel that remains trapped in the system after draining the fuel from the aircraft with the aircraft in level flight attitude. The weight of this residual fuel is counted as part of the empty weight of the aircraft.

Service ceiling. The highest altitude at which an aircraft can maintain a steady rate of climb of 100 feet per minute.

Small aircraft (14 CFR part 1). An aircraft weighing 12,500 pounds or less maximum certificated takeoff weight.

Standard empty weight. (GAMA) The weight of a standard airplane including unusable fuel, full operating fluids, and full oil.

Static load. The load imposed on an aircraft structure due to the weight of the aircraft and its contents.

Station. (GAMA) A location along the airplane fuselage usually given in terms of distance from the reference datum.

Strain sensor. A device that converts a physical phenomenon into an electrical signal. Strain sensors in a wheel axle sense the magnitude of the force the axle deflects and create an electrical signal that is proportional to the force that caused the deflection.

Structural station. A location in the aircraft, such as a bulkhead, that is identified by a number designating its distance in inches or percent MAC from the datum. The datum is, therefore, identified as station zero. The stations and arms are identical. An item located at station +50 would have an arm of 50 inches.

Takeoff weight. The weight of an aircraft just before beginning the takeoff roll. It is the ramp weight minus the weight of the fuel burned during start and taxi.

Tare weight. The weight of any chocks or devices that are used to hold an aircraft on the scales when it is weighed. The tare weight must be subtracted from the scale reading to get the net weight of the aircraft.

TEMAC. Trailing edge of the mean aerodynamic chord.

Type certificate data sheets (TCDS). The official specifications issued by the FAA for an aircraft, engine, or propeller.

Undrainable oil. The oil that does not drain from an engine lubricating system when the aircraft is in the normal ground attitude and the drain valve is left open. The weight of the undrainable oil is part of the empty weight of the aircraft.

Unusable fuel. (GAMA) The fuel remaining after a test has been completed in accordance with governmental regulations.

Usable fuel. (GAMA) The fuel available for flight planning.

Useful load. (GAMA) The difference between takeoff weight, or ramp weight if applicable, and basic empty weight.

Utility category. A category of aircraft certificated under 14 CFR part 23 and CAR part 3 that permits limited acrobatic maneuvers but restricts the weight and the CG range.

Wing chord. A straight line distance across a wing from leading edge to trailing edge.

Zero fuel weight. The weight of an aircraft without fuel.

Index

A

adverse-loaded CG checks.............................7-6
aft adverse-load CG check 7-7
aircraft category 4-3
aircraft certification.....................................4-3
aircraft classification 4-3
airplanes 4-5
airships 4-5
airworthiness certificate 4-4, 4-8
alteration 7-1, 7-5
amateur-built aircraft 4-3, 4-6, 4-8
amateur-built LSA 4-1
arm 2-2, 7-5, 10-5

B

balance 1-4
    control...1-4
ballast... 3-4, 7-7, 10-7
balloon... 1-5, 1-6, 4-5
basic empty weight 5-2, 6-2
basic weight and balance equation.................2-4

C

cargo...9-18
center of gravity 2-2, 3-1, 5-1, 9-1, 10-1
    change..7-1
    configuration...9-18
    determining 3-5, 10-4
    determining changes.................................. 9-6
    determining lateral CG of a helicopter.....................10-5
    determining the loaded CG..........................9-3
    limits envelope 5-4
    range 2-6
    range chart 2-10
certificates and documents 4-8
chart method.. 6-2, 6-3
Civil Aeronautical Administration....................2-6
civil air regulations 2-6, 3-4
commuter category.......................................9-1
commuter category airplanes 9-12

A

comprehensive equipment list......................2-10
computer 10-1
consensus standard..................................... 4-3
cyclic control.. 8-1

D

data pertinent to all model............................2-6
datum..3-7
    aft of the main wheels 3-7
    forward of the airplane 3-6
dedicated electronic flight computer.............10-3
determining cargo pallet loads 9-9
determining new balance point 2-3
determining weight 10-6
documenting changes...................................9-3
draining the fuel...3-4

E

E6-B flight computer............................. 10-1,10-2
effects of weight..1-3
electronic calculator 10-2
electronic load cells.....................................3-2
empty weight...9-2
empty weight center of gravity 3-2, 6-2, 7-6, 8-3, 9-2
empty weight CG range 2-6
equipment for weighing 3-2
equipment list............................... 3-4, 5-2, 7-2
EWCG formulas..3-6
experimental airworthiness certificate 4-6
extensive repair 3-2

F

FAA designee..4-4
finding balance point....................................2-3
fixed-wing airplane 1-5
fleet operating empty weights (FOEW) 9-5
floor loading limits......................................9-9
forward adverse-load CG check....................7-7
fuel capacity..2-6
fuel dump 9-12

G

gliders..4-1, 4-5

H

helicopter...1-5, 8-1

I

initial weight 9-2

J

jacking the aircraft 3-5
jacks 3-5

K

kit-built aircraft 4-6

L

landing gear shock struts......................3-5
landing weight......................................9-10
large aircraft..9-1
lateral balance 1-4, 8-2
lateral CG..8-3
lateral level...3-5
law of the lever...............................2-1, 2-2
leading edge 3-8
leading edge mean aerodynamic chord (LEMAC) 7-6, 9-2
leveling the aircraft 3-5
lift...1-2
light aircraft..1-5
lighter-than-air aircraft.....................4-1, 4-5
light sport aircraft (LSA) 4-1, 4-2, 4-3, 4-6
light-sport category 4-3, 4-4
light-sport eligible kit...........................4-3
load cell scales 3-2
loaded CG 6-2
    of a helicopter.................................8-3
loaded weight 6-3
loading graph method 5-4
locating balance point.....................2-2, 2-3
location of CG.......................................3-8
longitudinal CG.....................................8-3

M

major alteration 3-2, 7-3
manual computational method..............5-2
manufacturer-furnished information.......2-10
maximum amount of payload 9-10
maximum baggage................................2-6
maximum gross weight..........................1-6
maximum weights..................................2-6

mean aerodynamic chord 2-5, 3-1, 3-8
modifying the cargo 9-6
moment 2-2, 5-4, 7-5
    index.............................5-4, 7-5, 9-2, 10-5
    limits...6-3
multiengine aircraft..............................6-1

N

nosewheel airplane with datum ahead of the main wheels 10-4
nosewheel airplane with datum behind the main wheels 10-4
nosewheel landing gear.....................3-6, 3-7
number of seats 2-6

O

offloading cargo 9-6
offloading passengers............................8-3
oil 3-4
    capacity..2-6
onboard aircraft weighing system..........9-5
operational empty weight (OEW)...........9-5
other fluids 3-5
overloading 1-3

P

passengers 9-16
percent mean aerodynamic chord (MAC)......6-3, 7-6, 9-3, 10-5
permanent ballast 7-8
pilot in command 3-2
pilot's operating handbook 2-10
platform scales 3-2
powered parachute 1-5, 1-6, 4-1, 4-3, 4-5, 4-6, 4-8
preflight planning.................................5-2

R

ramp wheel scales 3-2
reestablishing the OEW 9-5
registration certificate...........................4-8
repair 7-1, 7-3, 7-5

S

safety 3-2, 3-5
scale preparation 3-3
shifting cargo 9-8
shifting the balance point......................2-4
shifting weight 2-4, 10-6
single-engine aircraft 5-1
solution by chart...................................2-4

special airworthiness certificate 4-4, 4-6
special light-sport aircraft (SLSA)............................4-5
stability...1-4
standard airworthiness certificate................................4-4
standard weights...3-4
statement of compliance 4-3, 4-5
stress panels 3-5
stress plates 3-5
Swept-wing airplanes..1-5

T

tailwheel airplane with datum ahead of the main 10-4
tailwheel airplane with datum behind the main 10-4
tailwheel landing gear 3-7
temperatures change..3-4
temporary ballast..7-8
    formula 7-8
total weight..9-2
trailing edge 3-8
trim setting 9-6
twin-engine airplane..6-1
type certificate data sheets 2-6, 3-8, 5-2, 7-6
typical placard...7-7

U

using fuel...8-3

W

weighing aircraft 3-2
weighing procedures 9-2
weight..1-2
    changes 1-3, 7-5
    envelope...6-3
    procedures 3-3

weight and balance..4-6, 4-8, 6-1
    computations 4-8
    control... 1-2, 3-2
    problems 10-4
    records 3-2
    record...7-3
    theory...2-2
weight and loading sheet..4-8
weight and moment indexes...6-3
weights 10-5
weight-shift control (WSC)................................... 4-1, 4-6
weight-shift control aircraft 1-5, 4-5, 4-6
wheels 10-4